'I'm a big fan of decluttering myself as I really believe it helps tidy the mind. I think what Nicola is doing is truly fantastic and her Instagram brightens up my day.'

KATIE PIPER

'TGCO is like having my very own Mary Poppins. She organises the chaos that enters my home on a daily basis and sprinkles her magic, making everything calm and tidy. She's changed my life …'

GEMMA COLLINS

'After I got sober, I realised that my house was in a state of barely organised chaos. It felt like the Old Curiosity Shop. Nicola came round, and with the magic that is her mind, reorganised the space I live in, making it look like the easiest thing in the world. Now my home actually relaxes me. I feel like Nicola has got the best out of it … and that, as a result, it gets the best out of me.'

BRYONY GORDON

'Nicola is my superhero, not all heroes wear capes.'

FERNE MCCANN

'Nicola's approach is relaxed, kind and, most importantly, in my opinion, achievable and sustainable. Let's face it, someone telling you to be tidier can get your hackles up, but Nicola's method is so different that you never feel as though you're being judged or shamed for having a chaotic knicker drawer or a disorganised bookshelf.'

EMMA GUNAVARDHANA

**Cleaning Your
Way to a Calm
and Happy Home**

# mind
# over
# clutter

## NICOLA LEWIS

**From the
creator of**
This Girl Can Organise

Thorsons

All names have been changed to protect client confidentiality.

Thorsons
An imprint of HarperCollins*Publishers*
1 London Bridge Street
London SE1 9GF

www.harpercollins.co.uk

First published by Thorsons 2019

13 5 7 9 10 8 6 4 2

A catalogue record of this book is
available from the British Library

ISBN 978-0-00-834482-5

Printed and bound in Great Britain by
CPI Group (UK) Ltd, Croydon, CR0 4YY

MIX
Paper from
responsible sources
FSC
www.fsc.org FSC™ C007454

This book is produced from independently certified FSC™ paper
to ensure responsible forest management.

For more information visit: www.harpercollins.co.uk/green

To Lottie, my beloved grandma;
to Valerie, my wonderful mum and
organising queen; and to Terry,
the best dad in the world.

# Contents

# My Journey

My name is Nicola Lewis. I'm 44, married to Graham and mum to two fabulous daughters, Amelia and Francesca, who are my absolute world.

I grew up in Walthamstow, in east London, but I now live in a village in rural west Essex, and I just adore my life. I love music and lip syncing (ha ha!), kindness and having fun, and living every single day to the full. But what I'm *really* passionate about – and what makes me tick – is organising and decluttering. In fact, I enjoy it so much that I've made it my business and my life's mission. And now I want to help you transform *your* life too and enjoy all the benefits that decluttering brings. Because This Girl Can Organise (TGCO) is all about getting stuff done – with a big smile on your face.

It all started eighteen years ago when I got my first job as an FX (foreign exchange) assistant working for an investment bank in London. I was literally over the moon and loved the idea of being a 'working girl', just like Melanie Griffith in the movie of the same name. I wanted the tailored suits and designer bags, the big hair, to be independent, earn my own money and, of course, have fun in all the clubs and bars. My career and salary grew over the years and I was proud to work for some of the biggest investment banks in the City of London.

However, it wasn't all plain sailing and I encountered a few storms along the way, especially when my first daughter was born. Don't get me wrong, my career was really important to me, but so was becoming a mum and all the changes that brings. Like most first-time mothers, I wasn't prepared for this transition, and not only were the back-handed comments from some of my colleagues after I returned to work hard to digest, they also made it difficult for me to focus. Holding down a full-time job while being a parent is never easy and it was probably one of the biggest challenges I've ever had to face. It was painful and I felt constantly guilty, trying to do the right thing and please everyone, which in reality was never enough, while constantly comparing myself to others. And although everything appeared to be OK on the outside, inside I was hurting.

The worst thing was that there was nobody I could confide in. I worried that if I talked honestly to people about what I was experiencing, I'd be labelled 'weak' and 'overemotional' and would be penalised accordingly.

I remember how, on some days, I would head into work feeling really positive, fresh and raring to go, only to find within minutes of arriving in the office that I had to choose between my career and my family. I felt guilty about leaving my family at home, but nobody really cared if you had a child in nursery or you'd snatched just four hours' sleep the night before – you just had to put on a brave face, carry on, accept your lot and be thankful that at least you had a good job. Even now it makes me feel sad writing this part of my story, and I wish I could go back in time and tell the young mum I was then that there was no need to worry and it would all turn out OK. However, I guess we all have to ride these emotions at some point in our lives.

Those first few years were very tough, and I felt as though I was slowly losing my identity and sense of fun. Every morning I would sit on the train on my way to work, writing lists and schedules. This enabled me to get everything out of my head on to paper and to plan ahead for the week, the month and even the year – anything just to help me smile, feel better about myself and give me something to look forward to. Inside, I felt trapped and I knew there had to be a better way to live, but my husband had just changed careers and was starting off as a freelancer in the entertainment industry and we desperately needed my salary to pay the mortgage and the bills. I felt that I had to make some sacrifices to help build a secure future for my family.

After the birth of my second daughter, I decided it was time for a change. I needed something new and exciting – something I would enjoy doing. So I swapped my old full-time job for a completely different part-time one as Ground VIP Customer Service Assistant for Harrods Aviation at Stansted Airport, looking after private and HNWI (high-net worth individual) clients. Yes, it was a bit random and involved a huge drop in my salary, but this career step was all about being happy and moving towards what the real me was interested in. So, I transferred my skill set from working on bustling trading floors to busy runways for the rich and famous.

For three years I enjoyed my work and had a lot of fun. I really loved meeting new people, being super-organised, professional and smart. Then one day I was approached by an old work colleague and offered a position at an investment bank in Canary Wharf with a big pay cheque and flexible hours. And it was part-time. The dream job, right? Well, actually, wrong. The moment I walked back into that open-plan office I knew I'd made a huge mistake. Yes, I had the right experience and qualifications, but I didn't have the passion or the drive. I was on autopilot, doing the job robotically, adhering to the bank's rules and regulations, and feeling miserable. What had I done?

I stayed for nearly two years and gave it my best shot. I kept trying to persuade myself that there was a place for me there and that's why I'd come back, but I guess I hadn't figured out what I really was good at and where my real talents lay. And that's the way it stayed until one blessed day when my whole team was called into the office – senior management and HR (human resources) at one end and the rest of us at the other – and it was announced that in December 2016 we would all be made redundant as our jobs were going overseas to India. And that was it! Strangely, I felt quite calm. It was almost a relief and I remember thinking to myself: this is God's plan; this is your time, Nicola, to really do something for you. You need to be happy and this is your opportunity to earn money doing what you love. I'd always told my children that we should only do what makes us happy and had never listened to my own advice, but now the time had come.

I felt liberated walking out of Canary Wharf that day and into the future. I was so excited to be leaving – finally, to have the opportunity to do something new and totally different. And although I hadn't a clue what that 'something' was, I knew that working in the City wasn't my scene and I needed a change. In my 20s it had all been about ambition, achievement and keeping up appearances, but it wasn't a healthy way to live. Now I had a family and I needed a better work/life balance. It's not always about the money and how we perceive worldly and material success. The time had arrived for me to be happy about my own life and to find out who I really was. I truly believe it was written in the stars. And since then, I've never looked back.

# Taking Control

It took a while for me to find my niche, to work out what I was going to do and how to go about it. I kept asking myself: 'What am I good at? What do I enjoy doing?' My husband suggested that as I loved organising things so much, why didn't I Google what's out there? I wanted to find something I really loved, and I knew I'd found it when I stumbled across an American website called *The Home Edit*, set up by two women who got paid to go out and help people organise their homes. Eureka! For years, whenever I used to pop round to friends, they would ask for advice on what they could do to improve their homes and, before I knew it, I was decluttering and organising them to create a better and happier living space. I loved doing it, but hadn't realised that it could be a real job.

When that day eventually dawned, it was a game changer. Now I knew this was something I could do well, in my own style – and make people happy. I knew that to take control of my life I needed to set up my own business and be my own boss. I wanted to create something that could help busy people who haven't the time or inclination to declutter by themselves, and so I set up my own website, blog and Instagram account on social media to motivate and inspire others, featuring real-life examples and case histories, complete with 'before-and-after' photos and practical advice and tips.

This Girl Can Organise was founded in April 2017 because I believed in myself, my skill set and my passion for organising and decluttering. It has grown and flourished and now, for the first time in my life, I feel in control. I love my work, running my business and helping other people to feel happier about their lives. And I have more time to devote to my own family and home too – I don't have to feel guilty any more. After all these years, I can finally feel good about myself and *be* myself. Every morning I wake up thinking: I can do this; and, what's more, I can have fun doing it.

*Before I knew it, I was decluttering*
*and organising to create a better*
*and happier living space.*

# My Passions

Organising is my big passion. Even when I was a little girl, I loved to arrange things. I guess I inherited my recycling and 'make-do' skills from my nan, Lottie, and my organising and life skills from my mum and dad, Valerie and Terry.

My nan was a huge part of my life. Flamboyant, bubbly, generous and kind, she donated and recycled tirelessly in her local community. She understood the needs and hardships of raising a family and was always thinking of others less fortunate than herself. Growing up, I would look up to her with such admiration. She showed me life's 'how-to-dos' with smiles and laughter. Her catch phrases were 'cleanliness is next to godliness' and 'make do and mend'. A stay-at-home mother, she raised six children on a tight budget and always kept an eye out for a bargain when she was shopping in the local markets. She was a great multi-tasker and just thinking about her still makes me smile. Not a day goes by without me missing her.

My mother, so caring and thoughtful, is the queen of organising, and I've learned so much from her. She loves to upcycle and donate, and this has made a huge impact on me and how I live my own life. While I was writing this book, I asked my parents whether I was always this organised and they both said, 'Yes, if it was on your terms!' They never had to tell me twice to clear up my room, as I always liked it to be neat and tidy. I'd play with my post office set or Barbie dolls and would always put them away inside their boxes because that was where they belonged. I guess it was all down to respect for my environment and being in my happy place.

I grew up in a tidy home, which was filled with love, and every Sunday from the age of 10 my sister and I helped our parents with household chores. We would clean or tidy our bedrooms, get out our school clothes and lay the table for dinner. My dad always took us to the park or swimming every Sunday morning so my mum could get her chores done and cook the dinner in peace – I only understand now as a mother how amazing that must have felt. Ha, ha! Both our parents worked while we were growing up, but they were always there for us. We had a routine for work, school and after-school activities and we all supported each other.

Although we didn't have masses of toys like children do today, and there certainly wasn't a special designated playroom, my sister and I were encouraged to be creative and to play anywhere. I loved reading books and writing in diaries, playing outside for hours on end and dancing and acting at my local stage school. I wasn't brought up with lots of material possessions, just what made me happy, and maybe this is where my passion for decluttering comes from. I believe that most of us have too much stuff; less really is more.

I'm also passionate about sustainability and the environment and I want my children to grow up in a better world where we preserve our natural resources, reduce the impact of global warming and enjoy cleaner air and water. Climate change is the biggest issue of our time, and while you might think that individually you can't make a difference, even tiny changes in your lifestyle can help.

*Most of us have too much stuff; less really is more.*

Living in a kinder, more thoughtful way is a good place to start and I try to do this in my own life. As a family, we've taken practical steps in our home to be more eco-friendly and to live our lives more sustainably. I buy smart and use environmentally friendly cleaning products that don't contain harsh chemicals, or I make my own with natural ingredients, such as essential oils, lemons, bicarbonate of soda and vinegar (see Chapter 3). I also recycle as much as possible, wage war on plastic and upcycle lots of common household items to give them a new, useful life (see Chapter 4).

# My Mission

Since starting my business, I've discovered my mission and my joy. I'd like to do some good in the world and for my career to have a sense of purpose, and I feel fortunate that I've met and helped so many lovely people whose lives have been transformed for the better by organising and decluttering their homes.

My blog and Instagram feed are full of helpful tips on how you can declutter, tidy, organise, recycle, upcycle, eco-clean and donate, and for a long time I've wanted to write it all down in a 'go-to' way that will help, inform and encourage people. And here it is. Packed with useful information and tips to motivate you and help you think more positively, this book will inspire you to get rid of all the clutter in your life and make it much simpler and happier.

You really can achieve anything you put your mind to. If I can do it, so can you.

# *10 ways to . . .*
# be happy and feel good

It's easy to feel good about yourself and your life if you start counting your blessings, follow your dream and get organised. Here are some ideas to inspire you:

## 1.

### DO WHAT YOU LOVE

There is a lot of truth in the sentiment that if you do what you love, you'll never work a day in your life. If you're unhappy and can't find a new job, try to shift your focus and look for the positives in your current one. At the very least, do one thing you enjoy every day.

## 2.

### FOLLOW YOUR DREAM

Dream big. Since starting TGCO in 2017 I have had the best time! I have met loads of incredible people, made some wonderful friends and have visited homes across the UK. I really believe that if you work hard and surround yourself with your dreams, they will one day come true (so start making that vision board – see p. 97).

# 3.

## STAY FOCUSED AND BELIEVE IN YOURSELF

You are already fresh and fabulous and can achieve whatever you put your mind to. Try to stay away from negativity and never forget your goals.

# 4.

## LIVE FOR EACH DAY

Life is short, so embrace every minute. Don't be held back by what has happened in the past. Be fearless and look for new opportunities and experiences.

# 5.

## GET UP EARLY

Those quiet moments in the morning are a great time to reflect on your life and what you want your day to look like. It also means you won't have to rush, and that will immediately make you less stressed.

# 6.

## GO FOR A WALK

Getting fresh air is a brilliant way to clear your mind and it is also a great opportunity to think and plan.

# 7.

## HELP OTHERS

Be compassionate and empathetic. Helping others grow is the best way to help yourself grow. Volunteering is one way to do this; or start with your friends and family and those around you.

# 8.

## SMILE

Every day is full of endless possibilities. You are in control of your attitude, so start your days with a smile and stay optimistic.

# 9.

## PLAN A TRIP

It's good to have something
to look forward to.

# 10.

## PRACTISE GRATITUDE

Be thankful for everything
you have already. Celebrate
the present and take a more
active role in your life.

A person's most useful asset is not a head full of
knowledge but a heart full of love, an ear ready
to listen and a hand willing to help others.
I believe these are the main qualities of TGCO.
Kindness is free, and it really does make the
world smile.

— ANONYMOUS CLIENT

# 1: Tidy Home,
## Tidy Mind

I love to have a clear, clutter-free space. Getting rid of all the clutter really is transforming and helps to clear my mind as well as the room I'm in, making me feel calmer and more relaxed; so 'tidy home, tidy mind' makes a lot of sense to me.

Decluttering gives you more time for yourself and your family and leads to a healthier and more balanced you. And although a clean environment won't necessarily solve all your problems, it can have an enormous impact on your emotional wellbeing and outlook and make all the difference to your life.

# What is 'Clutter'?

Clutter means different things to different people, but it's basically all about filling a space with an untidy and chaotic collection of things. It might happen for a positive reason, such as when you're moving house or you're decorating or renovating, or it may build up almost imperceptibly over time. If you find that you have to move things around in your home to accomplish a simple chore, or you feel that you're drowning in 'stuff' and overwhelmed by all the space it takes up, then the likelihood is that you have a clutter problem.

# Clutter and Mental Health

Your surroundings can have a dramatic effect on your mood, negatively impacting on your mental health – especially if you're stressed, under pressure or just struggling with the daily grind. Having unnecessary clutter lying around can act like a visual noise, each item potentially triggering an alarm bell in your head. The truth is that most of us have so much stuff either lying around in full view or shoved inside cupboards that it's sometimes impossible to find what we are looking for when we want it. With so much to do – laundry to wash, meals to prepare and paperwork to organise – it's no wonder that sometimes we feel overwhelmed when we're faced with the endless 'to-do' lists of life.

Studies in the United States[1] have looked at the causes of clutter and how it impacts people's emotional wellbeing. The researchers found that cluttered homes can be stressful to live in. Yet many people avoid reorganising their things and throwing out even unused or unwanted belongings, especially if it's time-consuming or unpleasant. Consequently, they sometimes end up living in a chaotic state, surrounded by mess, which can trigger a physiological response, usually in the form of stress and raised cortisol levels. Cortisol is the body's main stress hormone and when it increases it can lead to a variety of health problems, such as anxiety, headaches, fatigue, insomnia, memory lapses, concentration problems and even depression. When they declutter, however, even with small steps over a period of time, people can start to feel less anxious and better about themselves.

I know this is true from my own experience, from working with clients and from the feedback I get online in response to my blog and Instagram feed.

Elizabeth, a busy department manager who was diagnosed with depression and anxiety when she was 26 and had been off work for six months, struggled to stay on top of even basic everyday tasks like showering, cleaning the kitchen or vacuuming the carpets. She wrote to me:

> One day my mum offered to help clean my house and I was offended. Had it really got that bad? It made me realise I was truly debilitated by my illness. I felt so useless, but I know now that a lot of my untidiness was linked to self-worth and I didn't see myself as deserving of a clean and well-ordered home.

What Elizabeth learned from TGCO is that cleaning and decluttering needn't be a chore; it can be a pleasure if you approach it in the right way. You can make it more fun by including your family or turning on some music. Elizabeth saw it as her opportunity to catch up on her favourite podcasts and audiobooks and she felt so much better for getting up and moving around. She also valued the support of the TGCO community on social media:

Talking to people online about depression and anxiety has been a lifeline because I tend to isolate myself when I'm feeling low. But scrolling through Nicola's feed gives me a friendly nudge in the right direction and makes managing my home feel so much more attainable. There's no unrealistic standard to try to achieve, just moral support and helpful advice.

Elizabeth now looks forward to decluttering:

The biggest thing I learned is that I don't have to tackle mammoth tasks all at once, and that's very comforting. I don't worry about getting the whole house tidy. I just pick a small space and see where it takes me. Doing a little every day is much more powerful for my sanity, as well as my home organisation.

# The Power of Decluttering

I've witnessed many times the powerful effect that decluttering can have on my clients' state of mind. When I arrive at people's homes, they are usually very excited to see me (always a good sign!). Sometimes they tell me that this is the moment when they breathe out and start to relax; the task they've been dreading is about to be sorted once and for all.

You see, not everyone likes to declutter and get organised all by themselves. It can be, for some people, sheer drudgery if they don't enjoy doing it or are too busy to set aside the time. And it can be quite traumatic if people become over-attached to some of their personal possessions and find it hard to let go. I can help to reassure my clients by smiling, taking control of the situation and trying to make the process more fun for them. We will have a chat and a laugh together as we work. I encourage them to tell me what makes them feel relaxed when they're at home, and then, if they become overwhelmed, I can do something positive to help lighten the mood and take the stress out of what we're doing. It could be lighting a soothing candle, listening to the radio or a favourite playlist, enjoying some background cooking aromas, or just taking a break from the job in hand and sitting down for a chat with a cup of tea and some biscuits.

It's not rocket science – really, it's just about what makes you happy and what transports you to that happy place. And so decluttering becomes a part of your self-care routine and a way of taking care of yourself and your home.

*It's not rocket science. It's just about what makes you happy and what transports you to that happy place.*

# Asking for Help

Asking for help can sometimes be embarrassing or even scary. How many times have you said to a friend or relative: 'Let me know if there's anything I can do to help', but you never heard back from them? I guess some people see it as a sign of weakness or they feel insecure allowing someone to do something for them. There's no denying that we feel stronger and more in control when we fend for ourselves, but it's important to note that we are even stronger when we work together as a team.

When I started my business, I wasn't fully aware of the immense and transformative power of decluttering. I knew it worked for me, but I hadn't seen the wonderful effects on other people's lives.

One day I received a call from Sarah, who was desperate for my services and couldn't believe she had found someone who did exactly what she had been looking for. She was extremely emotional on the phone and I remember trying to reassure her and saying, 'Well done, you've just cleared your first hurdle by recognising you've got a problem and asking for help.' I couldn't wait to lend a hand.

Sarah and her husband both worked for a large law firm in the City of London and every day they both left the house just after 6am and didn't return until around 9pm. They loved their jobs, but the pressure was high. Sarah became increasingly anxious when the weekends came around and she opened the kitchen cupboards and wardrobes. Along with the bathroom and the living spaces in her house, they were full of stuff and she knew she had to sort it, but the problem seemed so immense and insurmountable that she couldn't psych herself up to tackle it. It was so overwhelming that it was even starting to affect her relationship with her husband and how she felt about herself. She compared herself unfavourably with some of her work colleagues who were in a similar situation but, unlike her, they just seemed to get on with it and sort out the mess.

Sarah's main reason for inviting me into her home was that she couldn't do it all by herself and she needed help. Together, we came up with a plan of which areas were in most urgent need of decluttering and got down to business. To her immense surprise and relief, we had so much fun. While we worked, she played songs by Prince, her favourite artist, and she sang, danced, cried, hugged me and stepped back in amazement – all because she could feel her worries disappearing as a huge weight was lifted off her mind.

This was when I truly realised the huge impact that decluttering can have and it made me excited and motivated to help even more people.

There's no need to feel guilty or harbour a sense of failure because you're asking someone else to help you declutter. It's often much more effective to hand a problem over to someone who isn't personally involved and can tackle it more dispassionately. It's all too easy to get sentimental and overemotional when you have to make decisions about ditching your belongings.

Comparing yourself to others is a natural thing to do, especially when things aren't going your way and if you have friends who appear to take it all in their stride. But you need to remember that we all lose our sh*t at times, and some of us just hide it better than others. As my grandma Lottie always used to say, 'The grass isn't greener on the other side; it's greener where you water it.' And how right she was! So let's all do our best not to compare and to embrace what we have. Be happy and never be afraid to ask for help or to offer to help others who need it. Most importantly, always be kind to *you*.

# Getting Started

Of course, you may not need me on hand to get started. You may feel that the time has come for you to roll up your sleeves and have a go yourself. So once you've decided to take the plunge, the key is to analyse the problem, figure out a plan and work through it gradually, one task at a time, embracing the process and going about it in an orderly, methodical way.

1.  Grab yourself a pad of paper and a pen and begin by writing a to-do list for every room in your home, noting down all the items you'd like to declutter from each one (more about this in Chapter 2).
2.  If you feel you need help, ask a family member or a friend. Feeling supported and getting a second opinion is beneficial and makes the whole process much easier.
3.  Once you've decided on a plan, set aside an hour a day or however long you can spare for decluttering and tick the jobs off your list as you go along, tackling one room at a time.

# One step at a time

Don't try to do too much too soon. If you do, at some point the task will overwhelm you and that could put you off continuing. Starting small is better than not starting at all. So take it a step at a time and celebrate the little 'wins' and positives as you go along. Don't rush it – this is a long-term, lifelong process, not a quick fix or makeover. Decluttering can radically change your life and lead to better, more sustainable habits and a new mindset.

Big challenges can be intimidating, so turn them into measurable goals – say, 30 minutes a day – and you'll be blown away by how much you can achieve. Start to self-love and self-praise: tell yourself you're doing your best. Then nothing is impossible.

**Don't be disheartened if it takes longer than you expected. Remember that even one tick is better than none. Decluttering can take time and there's no need to rush.**

# Take Back Control

By using my simple method you'll soon start to feel a sense of achievement and satisfaction as you take back control of your life and introduce more order into your home. This, in turn, will motivate you to move on to the next task or room and the time you spend decluttering will become a pleasure rather than a chore. My mum always says that it refreshes your home, your mind and your overall wellbeing, and she's right: you'll feel much happier living in an environment that isn't crammed with clutter and items you don't use. It's liberating and empowering to purge the stuff you don't want or need any more. It makes you want to smile and gives you the space to breathe, to be calm and to focus on what's important for you.

We all have too much stuff, and removing or reducing the number of items that no longer have any purpose and don't make you happy will give you untold satisfaction. It feels great to be happy with what you have and not feel the need to accumulate. Getting rid of personal belongings can be tricky, especially if they are associated with good memories, but there's no point hanging on to something just because you 'might need it some day'. If you haven't used it or worn it for years or it still has the original labels and tags attached, it's time to chuck it, even if you feel an attachment to it.

*Start to self-love and self-praise:*
*tell yourself you're doing your best.*
*Then nothing is impossible.*

# Saving things 'for best'

How many times have we all used the phrase, 'save it for best', whether it's fancy underwear, expensive shoes, a posh dress or the finest champagne flutes? And how do you know when 'best' actually is?

I've seen so many items in people's homes, especially designer handbags, shoes, belts and clothes, that don't get used or worn on a regular basis because they are being 'saved for best'. And when I ask my clients what that actually means, their answers usually focus on the items' cost.

When we're out shopping for 'best' items, we get excited about the whole experience: the location, the styling of the store, the service, the wrapping, handing over the money and the luxurious branded bag. These are all part of the company's plan to make us feel special and to enjoy our new 'best' item. However, once we bring it safely home, it all too often gets stored in a bag on a shelf in our wardrobe. Out of sight and out of mind.

Change this next time you treat yourself to something special: gaze at it and smile ... you've had a wonderful experience and now it's time to enjoy your purchase and show it off to the world. Every day should be your 'best' day, so use the good stuff you've worked hard for; have fun and enjoy wearing or using it to the full. As Kate, one of my clients, put it:

Imagine going shopping in the sales at a huge bargain-basement department store. There's stuff everywhere, but among all the confusion you find some amazing pieces. And you pick up things that would be perfect for your friends, family and charities – it feels so good to give. Afterwards, you go home, and everything is so calm and all the items you found are so beautiful and just right. You relax, but then you realise that you weren't charged for any of them. Having TGCO has made me take a fresh look at my home and all my treasures. I don't miss anything I've discarded or given away, and I feel so calm and grateful for everything I have. It's freed my mind to be creative again.

# It's OK to have a wobbly day

None of us is immune to a wobble – even TGCO has the odd moment. Life is full of highs and lows, but a wobbly day doesn't mean you're going down again. On the contrary: it's *just* a wobbly day and they happen to us all from time to time – you're not alone. Talking to someone (close friends and family can be very supportive), shedding a few tears or writing down how you feel can all help (as does my favourite – lemon meringue pie!). But try to keep things in perspective and remember what's important, and things won't seem so bad.

*Don't wait for a better today,
make today better.*

**TGCO Top Tip** If you can't allocate time every day to clean and tidy, don't worry. Find a decluttering solution that works for you and your daily routine. For example, tackle the small, achievable tasks first before moving on to the more difficult or time-consuming ones. Working in this way, you'll be able to tick more jobs off your to-do list and you'll feel really good about yourself and the progress you're making. You'll be back in control and you'll love living in your tidy home.

# Talk to a Life Coach

A cluttered life often brings lots of debilitating and negative emotions, including stress, guilt, confusion, shame, anger and self-judgement. It's disheartening if you feel like this every time you open the fridge, a cupboard or a drawer; or even when you look at your computer desktop or email inbox. We all live such busy lives and our mental load is hard enough to carry without these additional problems. In this chapter, I've made some of my own suggestions, but if you feel swamped and need help, talking to a life coach and working with them could make all the difference.

As Mary Meadows, an experienced life coach and NLP (neuro-linguistic programming) practitioner, says:

> Many of my clients choose to take part in decluttering. Whether they choose to declutter their phones from unused apps or their sock drawer of holey socks, I have yet to coach someone who hasn't uncluttered part of their life. A recent client shared with me that her sock basket was her nemesis: every morning when she looked inside it and found more pairs of socks needing sorting she thought, I am a bad mother. Every day those words were among the first things that went through her head. Through coaching around this subject, she was able to identify what it was that she needed to do, which patterns of behaviour had to be changed and, ultimately, how to change her perspective on that sock basket. Now she can laugh when it's mentioned and tells everyone she knows how coaching not only uncluttered her sock basket, but also how she now feels a new sense of confidence, resilience and optimism. It literally changed her life.

Decluttering a small area, whether it's a cupboard, a drawer or just your handbag, will support your mental health by not only giving you a sense of accomplishment, which is so important, but also creating space inside your head – space to let the good stuff in.

And it really can be a life-changer, as one of my online followers, Jennifer, can testify:

> Your Instagram feed has helped me massively, not just to organise my home but also my life. I live with my three children in a two-bedroom flat, which is

very hard to keep tidy, but I've managed it with your help. It's so reassuring to know that everything has its place and the children know where to put things. It's still a work in progress but I'm getting there. Without your tips and 'before-and-after' photos I would be living in a very cluttered, messy home.

*Remind yourself that it's OK not to be perfect.*

# The positive impact of decluttering

**Fiona Thomas, mental-health blogger and journalist**

In a study published in the *Personality and Social Psychology Bulletin* in 2009,[2] women who said their homes felt 'cluttered' were found to have higher levels of cortisol (the stress hormone) than those who described their homes as 'restful' or 'restorative'. Although cortisol is required for good health, excessive amounts in the body are associated with mood swings and irritability, which puts some people at a higher risk of suffering from depression and anxiety. They are less able to regulate common behaviours like concentration, decision making, judgement and social interaction, and although the link between depression and elevated stress levels is complicated, there is definitely a benefit in trying to reduce stress in order to improve overall wellbeing.

As a mental-health journalist, I encounter hundreds of people, online and offline, who are struggling to deal with depression and anxiety, and one of the universal problems is an inability to deal with an ever-growing list of things to do. Whether it's paying an overdue utility bill, mailing a letter or renewing a passport, many seem to find these everyday tasks near impossible. I know this is true because I've been there myself. I've worn dirty clothes for days because I can't bear to make a dent in a month's worth of laundry. I've shoved piles of unwanted books, shoes and mismatched bikinis under the bed and shamefully snuck under the duvet at two in the afternoon. I've let credit-card debt spiral out of control because I can't bear to pick up the phone to sort out my finances. It's a well-known fact that depressed people find it difficult to take care of, well, anything. And it's taken me years to realise that all of this clutter, mental and physical, can be tackled successfully in small steps.

In fact, taking that first tiny step in the right direction can give you the momentum to take the next one, and then the next, until, eventually, balance is restored and, before you know it, you'll have conquered a mountain of boring tasks, such as cancelling that out-of-date insurance policy and vacuuming behind the sofa.

The positive impact that decluttering can have on our minds should not be underestimated. This doesn't mean that a well-organised home will lead to infinite happiness, but taking control of your surroundings will most likely help you to feel more in control of life in general. Not only that, but studies have found that people who do simple tasks such as making their bed each morning are 19 per cent more likely to get a good night's sleep.[3] Depression is often the cause of sleep problems, and insomnia can make anxiety substantially more difficult to manage, so let me tell you first-hand that good-quality sleep is one of the simplest ways to address low moods at the onset of anxiety.

However, don't just take my word for it. I speak to people every day who have found taking control of their clutter has had a tangible impact on their mental wellbeing. For instance, one woman recently told me that tidying for just 10 minutes helped calm her mind and that putting each item back in its rightful home is representative of the mental burden she carries around all day. The act of having clear physical surroundings helps her mind feel just as organised. I've also spoken to psychologists who champion the soothing effect of clearing out when it comes to managing the symptoms of mental illness. One told me that the weight of responsibility we feel when we're overwhelmed is lightened, and it gives us a sense of mastery, action and pleasure which can alleviate the air of hopelessness that often accompanies depression.

Unfortunately, knowing that decluttering has an elusive healing power doesn't automatically mean that people with depression and anxiety can easily get on board. Feeling sluggish, tearful and unable to get out of bed is hard enough, so the seemingly small act of reaching for a duster can take days or even weeks of self-motivation to put into action. In the same way that exercise, a balanced diet and talking therapy can aid in recovery for mental illness, I can say with confidence that tidying up is just as important.

The great thing about TGCO is that there are no unrealistic standards to live up to. If all you managed to do was take out the bin today, then that's OK, because small steps lead to more steps and before you know it, you'll be standing in the light, feeling organised and ready to take on the world.

*Starting small is better than not starting at all.*

# 10 ways to . . .
## a tidy and calm you

Successful decluttering is all about being relaxed yet organised. If you feel in control and chilled about all the jobs you have to do, the task will not only be much easier, but also more enjoyable. Here are some tips and hints on how to have a tidy house ... and mind:

## 1.

### MAKE YOUR BED FIRST THING IN THE MORNING

It's a small accomplishment, but it will set the tone for the rest of the day. Your bedroom should be your sanctuary and a made bed will make it look put together and tidy. This will help you declutter your space and, in turn, your mind.

## 2.

### PLAN THE WEEK AHEAD EVERY SUNDAY

When you have a plan, you'll start each day with focus. Planning can reduce stress and will make you more productive. You'll feel more in control because you won't have to worry about what is happening tomorrow or the next day.

# 3.

## DO AN INVENTORY OF EVERY ROOM

You should know what you have in your home. While you're decluttering, make a list of everything important that is left in each room; that way you'll know when something isn't where it's supposed to be.

# 4.

## CHECK YOUR CUPBOARDS AND DRAWERS

It's so easy to stuff things into a cupboard or drawer and forget about them, but that is how clutter starts to build up. Carve out some time on a regular basis to get rid of anything old, expired or unnecessary and you won't feel as nervous when you open up that junk drawer.

# 5.

## IF SOMETHING DOESN'T MAKE YOU SMILE, THEN SAY FAREWELL

Surround yourself with things that make you happy. That dress that is two sizes too small and makes you feel bad every time you see it? Not worth keeping.

# 6.

## IF YOU NO LONGER HAVE A USE FOR SOMETHING, DISCARD IT

Raise your hand if you have chargers in your house for items you got rid of years ago ... Don't hoard things that you don't use regularly or even at all – they just take up space.

# 7.

## PUT EVERYTHING AWAY NEATLY AND TIDILY

Don't rush. Even though the mess may be overwhelming, you'll be glad in the long term if you give yourself time and work in an orderly manner.

# 8.

## PLAY SOME RELAXING MUSIC OR A PODCAST

If you dread a task, it helps to incorporate some fun into it, so that it feels less daunting. Dance around the room and act silly while you're tidying up and it will be over in no time. I love to lip-sync!

# 9.

## REMEMBER THAT ONE TICK ON YOUR TO-DO LIST IS BETTER THAN NONE

Break up your list into easily achievable tasks. There is a great sense of accomplishment when you cross things off, so make sure that you finish at least one thing each day, even if it's just making your bed.

# 10.

## PLAN YOUR REWARDS AND GIVE YOURSELF SOME 'ME' TIME

You can't take care of other people if you don't take care of yourself. Make sure you give yourself time to do things that make you happy and incentivise you. For example, reward yourself with a bubble bath after you've organised your kitchen.

# 2: How to Declutter:

## Room by Room

Your home should tell the story of who you are and house a collection of everything you love. It can inspire you to go out into the world and do great things, and then welcome you back into a calm, relaxed and happy place to recharge your batteries.

To start the decluttering process, I want you to walk around your home, room by room, and get inspired. Look carefully and critically at each room and ask yourself:

- How can I improve it?
- Can I manage the available space better?
- Is it working storage-wise?
- How can I declutter it?
- What sort of atmosphere and mood do I want – more spacious, effective and functional; exciting and motivational; or cosy, relaxing and calming?

Your overall objective is to create a calm and happy space that you feel good about coming home to – one that works for you, so you live happily ever after. Make the most of each room and it will make you smile every time you walk into it. Good things really do come from a tidy, decluttered home. By getting rid of the things and clutter you don't want and need, you can embrace the belongings that bring you joy.

Analyse the rooms individually, while remembering that they all fit together into a bigger picture. Think about the sort of mood and environment you want to create in your home as a whole.

# It's Easy Peasy

The TGCO Decluttering Plan is simple. You need to declutter first to organise later. Here are the four essential steps to transforming your home – and your life.

## 1. Remove

Collect all the items in the room – and I mean *all*.

## 2. Sort and purge

Place the items in four piles:

- Keep
- Donate
- Bin
- Sell

Review all the items in each pile and only keep the ones you use on a daily, weekly or monthly basis, plus those you really love. This is the time to be ruthless and to let go of all the broken, old things you've stuffed into a cupboard or drawer, out of sight and out of mind. And get rid of the stuff you bought on sale because it was a 'bargain' or 'might come in useful one day' but has never been used. If it's still in the original wrapping with the label or tags, the chances are you don't need it, so get shot of it now. If your cupboards and drawers are filled with unused surplus items, it will be impossible to stay organised and soon the mess will be everywhere, and you'll have to start tidying up all over again.

# 3. Clean

It's now time to clean the room and remove all traces of dirt and dust from the whole area. And don't just focus on what's visible on the outside; attack the cupboards, drawers and those high shelves, too, that are usually invisible. Pull out furniture and clean behind and below it. You want everything to be really clean before you start work on the next step.

# 4. Organise

Once the room is clean, it's time for the final step: to put things back and start organising. When your belongings are stored and tidied away your home will be more appealing. It will look clean, neat and calm and that will make *you* feel happy.

# You'll feel great

Whenever I go through the decluttering process with my clients I compare it to an exercise class. You start off really energised and raring to go, then you hit the middle part and that's when you start to check your watch and wonder when it will end and why you started. But by the time you get to the end, wow: you feel great, you're blown away by what you've achieved and you want more!

*Keep the items that make you smile and discard the ones that don't ... it's that simple.*

# How Often Should You Declutter?

Well, it's up to you and how messy your home is, but I recommend you make lists of what you need to do every day, once a week and once a month, plus seasonal and annual tasks. For example, you'll need to do things like making the beds every day; but some jobs, such as cleaning the bath, may only need to be tackled once a week, and others, like sorting out your spring, summer, autumn and winter wardrobe, can be done on a seasonal basis. This will make your life a lot easier and will dramatically reduce the time needed when the next tidying-up job arises.

**TGCO Top Tip**

There are lots of great ways to get rid of the items that you don't use. You could donate them to charity, sell them on an auction site, pass them on to someone you know who will benefit, or simply dispose of them. Decluttering these items will make room for the ones you do use.

# Declutter Your Bedroom

The perfect bedroom should be a sanctuary where you can unwind and escape from the daily grind. It should be a relaxing space, free of clutter, with no clothes strewn across the floor or piles of paperwork, gadgets or kids' toys. If you want your bedroom to be peaceful and tranquil, you can do without these distractions. They need to be tidied away, moved to another room or discarded.

*A stylish aesthetic, while keeping the mood calming and gentle, will make you smile every time you open the door.*

# Getting started

Your bedroom will feel more spacious and welcoming if it's clutter-free and everything has its own place. It will be easier to keep clean and tidy too, so you'll spend less time on household chores. It's a special and very personal room in your home that often gets overlooked because you (and your partner) are the only people who go in there. Because it's not on show and may only be used for sleeping, there's a tendency to think it doesn't matter as much as other rooms in the house. I think that's wrong. If you can create a stylish aesthetic while keeping the mood calming and gentle, it will make you smile every time you open the door. You'll feel more relaxed, less stressed and sleep will come much easier.

Following the four steps of my Decluttering Plan (see p. 40), start off by clearing out anything that doesn't belong and bin or donate any items you no longer need. Focus on what you want to keep and how best to store it all in your wardrobe, chest of drawers or bedside cabinets.

## Every day

Some tasks can't be put off for later or tomorrow. I make my bed first thing every morning. I see it as the first achievable task of the day. I enjoy plumping up the pillows, smoothing out the creases in the sheets, shaking the duvet and misting it all with some soothing aromatherapy linen spray. This may sound like a lot of work, but it takes me all of five minutes, it makes me feel good and I always smile seeing it looking so calm and inviting when I come home in the evening at the end of a long day's work.

## Every week

I change my bed linen once a week on a Sunday. This works for me because it's the weekend and I'm home to strip the beds, load the washing machine and get everything dried and ironed. And there's nothing nicer than snuggling into bed on a Sunday night between crisp, clean sheets. It really is one of life's best feelings.

# DIY linen spray

It's so simple to make your own fragrant linen spray. You don't need to buy expensive fancy products and it's much healthier and more natural than using commercial brands containing chemicals.

You will need:

Distilled water
10 drops lavender essential oil
2 tbsp vodka

Mix everything together in a small spray bottle and shake well before use. Spray onto your sheets and pillowcases before you get into bed for a relaxing and restful night's sleep.

# Storage solutions

Effective storage is so important in your bedroom. Keeping everything tidy and clear of mess helps you to chillax and clears your mind.

Start by analysing the storage you've already got and whether it's working for you. It's surprising what you can achieve, even if it's not an especially large room. If there's limited storage in a bedroom, I always look for clever solutions and recommend you consider the following ideas:

- **Under-bed storage** is so useful, whether it's drawers in a divan base, a lift-up mattress bed or just plastic boxes that slide neatly underneath. Any of these options will give you ample space to store your bed linen, towels, PJs or even shoes or handbags.
- **Storage ottomans and vintage trunks** can be placed anywhere in the room or even double up as bedside tables. They look wonderful and are so useful for tidying away things like magazines, study materials, gift bags and shoes. Instead of cluttering up your bedroom floor, dressing table, chairs and other surfaces with all these items, arrange them neatly inside the trunks.

# Your bedside table

I don't know about you, but my bedside table gives me a sense of satisfaction and calm. It's home to all the things that keep me cosy, relaxed and ready for bed. I love getting into bed knowing that everything I need before I go to sleep is organised and all in one place close at hand.

Once a month, tidy up the tabletop and go through any drawers or shelves underneath, especially if you're one of those people who just shoves things in to make the room look neater, ignoring the mess within. Use small containers to arrange and house the important stuff. It's not the best feeling opening a drawer to a sea of mess, especially in the evening when you're feeling tired and want to chillax, so keep it organised and full of calm.

# Your drawers

Here's a test for you. Open the drawers in your wardrobe or chest and look inside. Does everything look neat and tidy, so you can find what you want quickly and easily? Or has it all been shoved in higgledy-piggledy and you are faced with piles of chaos stacked on top of each other, not knowing where anything is and feeling overwhelmed, your heart sinking when you look inside? If so, you need to get tough and take everything out. Go through it all, discarding what you don't need, and then come up with a plan for putting everything else back neatly in a way that works for you.

## Dividers

I love using dividers – they are a great way to organise drawers and create a home for each category, such as underwear, socks, tights, T-shirts, jumpers and gym wear. I like to roll clothes and place them neatly in rows within the dividers, but you can fold them if you prefer. This method allows you to see at a glance exactly what's inside. Plus, it makes putting away clean clothes a joy because everything has its place and is contained. You can even arrange items by colour.

**TGCO Top Tip**

When you empty your drawers, don't forget to clean them before you return everything. It's a nice idea to line them with some scented drawer liners, too, to make them look pretty and smell fresh. You can buy these or make your own. Just cut the lining paper to fit, allowing a little extra to fold up on each side and then mist lightly with the DIY Linen Spray (see p. 45) or make up a different one using another essential oil, e.g. rosemary, orange, nectarine or rose.

## Your wardrobe

Your wardrobe is not only a place for hanging your clothes, but also for storing all manner of things from boots and shoes to bags and accessories. So it's easy to see how it can quickly be overrun with clutter and why just opening the doors to remove your coat can overwhelm you. If this is the effect your wardrobe has on you, the time has come to declutter and sort it out.

All the hard work will be worth it when your wardrobe is organised and functional. You'll be able to find any outfit with ease, and you'll feel more excited about wearing your clothes when you can see the choices available without having to hunt for items that have fallen off their hangers. You'll feel so relieved when it's done and the fog clears. Best of all, you'll feel physically lighter and have more mental clarity. It's like a detox – you'll be in control, calmer, focused and on top of the world.

Go on, give it a go.

## One step at a time

To make the task easier, why not add the TGCO touch and put on some of your favourite music or something that will make you smile. You'll be amazed at how much fun cleaning out your wardrobe can be when you're in the right mood. I always encourage my clients to do this and sometimes we even sing or dance while we work!

1. Start by removing everything from inside the wardrobe. It helps to work in categories, placing each one in a particular area. So, you could remove all the hanging clothes and transfer them to a freestanding clothes rail or lay them out on your bed. Place all the shoes and boots on the floor, and sweaters, accessories, bags, etc. in another area.

2. Go through all your clothes and only keep the ones you love and that make you smile. Be ruthless when decluttering your wardrobe. Get rid of those ill-fitting jeans and anything you haven't worn in the last two years. Keeping skinny clothes is great if you've set yourself a goal, but if it's not going to happen, get rid of them. Likewise, sale bargains are fab if you need them, but if they still have their tags attached and are gathering dust, ask yourself whether you will ever wear them.

3. Start placing the items in four piles: keep; donate; sell; bin. Don't be tempted to skip this – it's a very important part of the decluttering process, so do try to stay on track and keep to this method.

4. Once you've bagged up the items you're not keeping, it's time to vacuum, dust and clean the wardrobe before you return everything else to it.

5. Think carefully about how you're going to organise everything. There are no hard-and-fast rules about this. It's what works best for you. Here are some options for you to consider:

- **Colour coordinate your clothes:** this is a great way to establish what you do and don't have in your wardrobe. If you end up with a sea of navy, black and grey, you might decide when you're next out shopping that perhaps the time has come to invest in some brighter shades to spice up your look. Alternatively, you may realise that these are the only colours you really like wearing, so it's pointless investing in anything bolder.

- **Organise in categories:** you may prefer to hang all your coats, dresses, shirts, skirts, etc. together in groups according to type for easy at-a-glance access. Trousers and jeans can be carefully folded over hangers or stored neatly in cupboards and drawers.

- **Seasonal order:** if you have a large wardrobe with plenty of hanging space, you'll have the luxury of hanging everything up in seasonal order, working from spring at one end through summer and autumn to winter at the other. Make sure you give yourself enough room to be able to see the clothes for each season – don't jam them in. If you don't have much space, you can hang up the things you are currently wearing and store the rest in vacuum bags that pack down flat.

*It's like a detox ... you'll be in control, calmer, focused and on top of the world.*

**TGCO Top Tip**

If you don't have space in your wardrobe to hang the clothes you're not currently wearing, store them in a clean, cool, dark and dry location until they come back into season. Do *not* place them near a heat source or anywhere damp.

## Which hangers?

There are many sorts of hangers, and the ones you use will not only help to keep your clothes in shape, but may also take up less space in the wardrobe – so consider your choices wisely:

- **Slim velvet hangers** are great for shirts, dresses and women's jackets and blazers. They give you so much room inside your wardrobe.
- **Wooden hangers** are best for men's coats and suits, but too many of them can become bulky and take up too much space.
- **Wooden clamp hangers** will keep skirts and trousers free from creases and don't take up much room. Plastic clip hangers are an alternative, but they can leave indentations on your clothes.
- **Coloured hangers** are fun, but think about which colour is best. White tends to show the dirt; black will show the dust. Grey; at least 50 shades are available, so find the right one for you.
- **Matching hangers** are the finishing touch. I like to match slim hangers throughout the wardrobe; it gives the space the final wow factor.

**TGCO Top Tip**

To prevent those pesky moths from attacking your clothes, fill linen drawstring bags with a handful of dried lavender, then hang them inside your wardrobe and place them in drawers. You can also buy special Ziploc plastic bags for storing any precious items of clothing, like cashmere sweaters, for example.

## No time?

Well, there's no time like the present but if you really don't have much time or feel overwhelmed by the prospect of tackling your whole wardrobe in one go, then just do a small section at a time. Start with your jumpers or your trousers, then move on to the next section when you're ready. Take it in small steps and you'll be proud of what you've achieved. And when you open the doors and see the improvement in one area, you'll be inspired to move on to the next.

**TGCO Top Tip**

Even if you've done an amazing job of organising your wardrobe, it will still need regular maintenance as you acquire more clothes, others wear out or fashions change. So make sure you revisit on a seasonal basis.

## Sorting out shoes

Shoes are a key component in any wardrobe, but how do they seem to have a life of their own and spread themselves randomly all over the house? They can be found in the porch, under the stairs, in the utility room, the entrance hall and the living room, as well as the bedrooms.

TGCO recommends that you gather up all your shoes and put them together, so you can review them and declutter:

1. Start by selecting your favourites. This process may quickly cut your collection in half: shoes that are keepers and shoes to donate or sell (if they have never been worn or are in good condition) or simply ditch. There's no point hanging on to pairs that have long outlived their usefulness or are past repairing.
2. Ask yourself these questions while you're decluttering:
   • When was the last time I wore these shoes?
   • Am I holding on to this pair 'just because …'?
   • Even if they look nice, are they killers to wear?
   • Am I willing to keep them at the expense of my limited storage space?
3. If you happen to come across a solitary shoe, all on its lonesome, place it in an open basket. The mate-less shoe will instantly be contained, and you won't have to worry about it for now; you can search for its twin at a later date.
4. Neatly place the shoes you wish to keep in the appropriate place in the wardrobe. Organise them by colour or heel height or category, e.g. trainers and exercise shoes, everyday, work shoes and evening shoes.
5. If you don't have much wardrobe space for storing your shoes, be creative. A glass cabinet can easily double up as a shoe closet and will provide a wow factor in your room. Beautiful shoes can look great arranged on shelves in a colour coordinated way or you can purchase a special shoe

rack or shoe organiser, or even repurpose and upcycle an old wine crate. There are so many ingenious ways of storing them – from wicker baskets to hanging them on ladders. Alternatively, you can avoid overcrowding by showcasing your seasonal and favourite footwear and storing the rest, which gets worn only occasionally, in clear shoe-storage boxes.

**TGCO Top Tip**

As well as organising your shoes and keeping your collection neat and tidy, look after them to keep them looking good and lasting longer. Always fit them with shoe trees to keep their shape and prevent them developing creases. Boot shapers will keep knee-high boots in shape for longer. Clean them regularly and check periodically to see if they need re-heeling or soling.

**TGCO Top Tip**

Keep your trainers clean and in good condition by cleaning them regularly. Scrub them gently with warm, soapy water, using an old toothbrush, and pat dry. Fill them with kitchen paper or rolled-up newspaper and leave to dry naturally. Crumpled-up newspaper is also an effective odour-eater, and once it's done its job, you can simply throw it in the recycling bin.

## Bedroom to-do list

- Make your bed every morning.
- Hang your clothes up whenever you take them off.
- Put your shoes away neatly in the designated place.
- Check drawers and cupboards regularly and keep them tidy.
- Air the bedroom every day to keep it smelling fresh.
- Light a fragrant candle in the bedroom to relax.

*Buy less. Choose well. Display what you love. Make it last.*

# Declutter Your Children's Bedrooms

If there's just one part of the house that we wish could magically tidy itself, it would probably be our kids' bedrooms, especially if they double up as a playroom, study and den. Thanks to the constant introduction of new books, toys, clothes, toiletries and all the other clutter that children accumulate, whatever their age, these rooms seem to get messier and more out of control by the day.

If your heart sinks every time you open the door and walk into your child's bedroom, don't despair, TGCO can help you to declutter it and offer some storage solutions and practical advice on keeping it tidier in the future.

Children are always going to play and make a mess, and of course we want them to be creative, to explore and use their imaginations. However, if you can get them on board and make tidying their rooms and putting their things away fun rather than a chore, you'll establish good habits that last a lifetime. The way you go about this is all-important, and you will be far more successful if you can motivate and reward them or, in the case of toddlers and younger children, turn the process into a game instead of barking out orders. This will defuse any tension, help to instill a sense of independence and achievement and make all your lives easier and more harmonious.

Some children are adamant that they can't let anything go and will throw a wobbly when you attempt to organise their space with them. However, if you reassure them by starting with only one drawer or a box at a time, it will help them to learn the process for themselves and establish a positive attitude towards decluttering, instead of hoarding everything they own under their beds for ever.

## Involve your kids from the beginning

It's so important to get your children involved from the earliest possible age when it comes to tidy-up time as they really will feel a sense of ownership sorting out their own stuff. You'll be teaching them a life skill, which they'll continue to use into adulthood. Work with them and not around them, getting them to understand how important it is to look after things and respect their belongings. They have to do it at school, so why not at home too?

How you go about it and phrase your requests can make all the difference between success and failure. Children don't react well to 'Just put it away' or 'Tidy up this mess *now*'. This is not only very negative, but also difficult to achieve, when half the time they don't know where to put things. It can make them feel that they are being punished because you're angry with the mess and this can lead to them perceiving tidying up as an unpleasant task rather than something they would do naturally. So, try changing how you ask them to do it:

- 'Do you want this item to live in this cupboard or this drawer?'
- 'Where is its home?'
- 'Shall we label these boxes, so you know where your things are?'

By motivating them to tidy up and doing it in a friendly, enjoyable way, you will encourage your children to be more enthusiastic and they will want to help. This will show them you respect their space, so they feel more involved, which will make tidying up more personal. You could get them to make labels and colour them in, or paint or decorate boxes and containers for housing their toys.

**TGCO Top Tip** Make the tasks you give your children age-appropriate. Only ask them to do things that are achievable and make them feel good about themselves.

## Getting started

When I work with children, I always get them to show me around their rooms before I start the decluttering process. This helps me to understand what's important to them and also what they don't like, and it is a good way to build a relationship of mutual trust. I like to be on their side, so they feel comfortable letting me know what they want to keep and what can go, even though they know a parent will come and review the situation.

Here are a few guidelines to get you going if you are doing this with your own child and a room that is spiralling out of control:

1. Start by removing everything that doesn't belong in the room, including cups, plates and dirty clothes.
2. Get out all the toys and books and sort them into categories, such as soft toys, educational and learning toys, games and puzzles, etc.
3. Ask your child to help you decide which toys they want to keep and put those away in a specially designated place or container, such as a laundry basket, box or bin. Your child can then help you to decide what goes where and you can label them together.
4. Encourage them to throw away any broken toys and items that no longer work, and to donate or give away toys they don't want or have outgrown. Instead of just removing things arbitrarily, use positive language – such as, 'Let's give this item a new home where another little boy or girl could play with it or use it'. Then they can feel good about themselves.
5. Teach them to put things away and perform basic cleaning tasks. They can help hang up their clothes, put used ones in the laundry basket and even vacuum the carpet. Make it fun, so they enjoy helping you and want to do it again.

Decluttering is overwhelming for adults, so it's no surprise that children feel the same when they're confronted with the challenge. To make it easier, I always break up the bedroom into zones and work on one at a time, especially with young children who may have a short concentration span and get bored easily. Let them make the decision on what stays and what goes, then you can clean and organise the area together afterwards.

## Storage solutions

There's no point in insisting that your children keep their bedrooms neat and tidy if you don't provide containers and special places for storing their things. Here are some ideas to inspire you:

- Use wicker baskets for storing some toys in category order, clothing, accessories or even shoes.
- Floating or built-in shelves are a storage lifesaver, especially in small rooms, and are perfect for small toys, frames and trinkets.
- Provide shelves or bookcases for books.
- Beds with built-in drawers underneath can be a good place for storing bed linen, toys, shoes or seasonal clothes.
- Put Lego and puzzles in clear containers or bags and label them clearly. This way, your kids can see the contents and can put things back in their place easily.
- If your children collect small items and miniatures, store them in stackable clear containers with flip lids. This makes them easy to open and, again, they can see at a glance what's inside.

# Puzzles, jigsaws and board games

We all love to play with these, adults as well as kids, but as soon as a piece is lost and you can't complete it, there goes the puzzle or game. Often, the boxes these things come in are not only very bulky and take up lots of space, but are also quite flimsy and pieces fall out. This problem is easily solved by making a special bag for each board game or puzzle. You will need:

A large clear Ziploc food bag
A pair of scissors
A permanent marker pen

1.  Write the name of the game or puzzle on the front of the bag.
2.  Empty the contents of the puzzle or game into the bag.
3.  Cut out the picture from the lid of the original box and place it inside, together with any instructions or rules, if appropriate. This allows everyone to see what each puzzle is and acts as a guide for assembling them or playing the game in question.
4.  Zip up the bag and place it in a container for games and puzzles.

This simple solution enables you all to find anything you want with ease. And when it comes to tidying up, you simply drop everything back in its bag, zip it up and put it away.

**TGCO
Top Tip**

Young children love routine and structure, especially when it comes to learning and play activities. So instead of letting them get out every toy and puzzle in the house and making a mess all over their bedroom floor (and every other area, too), encourage them to get things out one at a time. When they've finished with it, have fun picking up all the pieces and looking under rugs and furniture in case any have gone astray before replacing them in their own special bag (see box, p. 60). You'll feel good knowing that what comes out and what goes away is organised.

# Memory boxes

It's a good idea to get a small- or medium-sized memory box for each child's bedroom, in which to keep safe the things they want to keep or can't bear to be parted from, but don't want out on display. Photos, artwork, cards and things they have made or found often make it into the box and will be admired a lot more by being kept in a special place. Once or twice a year they can review what stays and what can go. It's important for both of you to go through this process together, so they feel they have control over their things. Ask them whether each item is special and needs to be kept and let them make their own decision – after all, it's their memory!

**Note:** if you're holding on to items of sentimental value that your child has moved on from, remove them from the room. It's you who wants to keep them for the memory and not your child, so save it in your own memory box.

*Work with your children and not around them, getting them to understand how important it is to look after things and respect their belongings.*

## Kids' wardrobes

I've encouraged my children, from an early age, to put their clean washing away by themselves. I believe that this is an essential skill set – a sign of independence that they can manage this by themselves without someone else doing everything for them. And once a month we go through their wardrobes together to see:

• Which clothes they aren't wearing.
• Which they might still need.
• What they've grown out of.

This is not only a great way to tidy up their wardrobes, it's also an opportunity to get out or put away seasonal clothes.

## Down to business

1. Start by taking out all the hangers. You can put them on a freestanding rail, lay them on the bed or even take them to another room for now.
2. Next, remove things that don't belong inside the wardrobe – anything that may be better stored elsewhere or put away for another season, or that needs washing, cleaning or mending.
3. Give the empty wardrobe a good clean or dust.
4. When you return the clothes to the wardrobe, organise them in category order to make it easy for your children to find what they need, e.g. school uniform, shirts, dresses, trousers, etc.
5. Give shoes a designated place, depending on the available space. You can arrange them inside the wardrobe or put them in baskets, on a shelf or in an over-the-door hanger, whatever works for you. Just make sure that you teach your children always to put them away into their place. Everything has a home.
6. When it comes to bags, sunglasses, belts and hair accessories, put these away in labelled clear boxes. This will minimise clutter in the room and keep the wardrobe looking tidy.

## Children's bedroom to-do list

Encourage your children, when they're old enough, to take responsibility for their own space and to keep it looking nice. Tidying and cleaning it at least once or twice a week will make them feel more grown up and in control. Depending on their age, they can:

- Make their bed every day.
- Pick up clothes from the floor and hang them up or put dirty ones in the laundry basket.
- Pick up shoes and put them away in pairs in their designated place.
- Put toys away in the boxes provided.
- Put books away on the shelf or bookcase.
- Collect any chocolate wrappers, sweet papers, packaging, empty cans and bottles lying around and throw them away in the bin or recycling container.

# Declutter Your Bathroom

How well organised is your bathroom? For me, a neat and clean bathroom is a joy to behold. It's a relaxing, calm place where I love to be, looking after myself or getting ready for the coming day. Plus it's easier to keep clean and I can declutter on a regular basis as I can see at a glance what's run out and needs replacing and what's expired. No matter how large, small, awkward or unusual your bathroom may be, you can take some basic steps to make it as clutter-free and functional as possible.

# Getting started

1. Take a deep breath and start by collecting all the items in the bathroom and sorting them into categories.
2. Go through everything and decide what you're going to keep, discard or replace. Grab yourself a black plastic bag and be ruthless. Throw away any empty shower-gel bottles, old razors, used-up toothpaste tubes and odds and ends of used bars of soap. You'll probably find a lot of containers with just a little body lotion or moisturiser nestling at the bottom. They take up a lot of space and if you've already moved on to another bottle, you're unlikely to use them now, so clean and recycle them.
3. When you've gone through everything (see p. 69 for medications), you can start to organise the area. To make this simpler and less daunting, divide the room up into zones – cupboards, drawers, shelving, the sink, shower and bath areas – and tackle them one at a time.

# Storage solutions

Depending on the set-up of your bathroom, you need to consider which storage products are going to work best in the available space. Containers, wall-mounted concealed cabinets, trunks, shelving and under-sink storage will all work wonders.

- If you have a lot of bulky items and towels, then a cabinet, shelving unit or chest is probably best.
- Installing floating shelves is one of the best ways to create additional space.
- Plastic or wicker containers that colour-match the room are a great budget option and will provide a safe home for clutter.

- A good storage organiser is particularly useful as it will maximise the space in the bathroom, while reducing the time you spend looking for items.
- You can also use doors for storage: hang towels or dressing gowns on the backs of doors, adding hooks for toiletry bags containing cloths, sponges and soaps. (You can use self-adhesive hooks for this, and they don't require any drilling.)
- In a shared bathroom, use coat hooks instead of a towel rail to prevent towels getting muddled up. You could even add initials to help the children put their towels back in the right place.
- Use containers to organise all the items you keep in the bathroom and to store them tidily. Divide them into categories, such as haircare, skincare, grooming tools, bath and shower products, body lotions and moisturisers, make-up, medications and bathroom cleaning products.

**TGCO Top Tip**

My top organising accessory in the bathroom is the clear container. When you go into a shop to buy your beauty, skincare and cosmetic products they are always arranged in neat rows to make them clearly visible. So why do we hide them away inside a drawer or throw them into cupboards to be forgotten for months? Now's the time to give them a fabulous new home: a clear container will allow you to organise your products so they can be seen and used every day – no more time-wasting first thing in the morning when you're looking for the tweezers or that new mascara.

# Make-up

A lot of us think twice before throwing away make-up. After all, most brands are quite expensive, and you always think it will come in useful one day. However, like everything else, if you don't use something or it doesn't add value, then there is no point in letting it clutter up the place.

## Getting started

1.  Empty all the make-up products out of your bathroom cupboards, shelves and drawers. (And your toiletry bag, handbag and anywhere else you might keep make-up.) Take all the products out of the room and put them on the kitchen or dining-room table where you can see them clearly. This also enforces a time limit on the decluttering process, as you'll probably need to use the table later in the day.
2.  Sort your make-up into categories, such as foundation and powder, lipsticks, mascara and eye shadow, etc. This helps you to identify what you have too much of and where you are over-purchasing.
3.  How old is your make-up? Check the expiry dates. (The recommended shelf life of most products is between six and twelve months.) Throw away any items you've opened that are way past their date or have got sticky or clogged up. Old make-up can harbour germs and cause skin irritations, so don't take the risk – get rid of it.
4.  Now it's decision time. Consider whether you are really going to use the remaining items. Go through them, one at a time, and ask yourself 'When was the last time I used this?' and 'Will I ever use it again?' Be ruthless, especially with last year's trendy colours and shades.
5.  Give everything that you're going to keep a good clean: the containers, cases, brushes, tweezers and make-up drawers.

6. Put everything back neatly, clean and tidy in a special box, container or drawer where you can find it all easily.

## Make-up storage solutions

Store your make-up where you can see it. Clear perspex containers are great as they help to separate all your beauty products and enable you to see what you have. You can store things in category order, plus it will make getting ready to go out more enjoyable as you won't be wasting time hunting for small items. Place them on a shelf or inside a drawer or bathroom cabinet. If you have a large make-up collection, it might be worth considering buying a special shelving unit or even a trolley to accommodate it.

TGCO
Top Tip

Store make-up brushes separately, bristles up, and clean them regularly. You can spray them with a special cleaning liquid to keep them clean, prevent a build-up of make-up residue and prevent potential skin problems.

# Hoarding

Don't hoard free samples: they are one of the biggest culprits for clutter. We collect them from hotels, stores and magazines, but rarely get around to using them. I've worked with clients who have whole baskets full of them – unused, gathering dust and well past their expiry dates.

Instead, donate any unused in-date samples to women's charities that can make good use of them.

## The medicine cupboard

A well-organised medicine cupboard will save you time and money, as well as making your home safer. Perhaps here more than anywhere, never underestimate the power of clearly labelled containers, as in the event of a first-aid incident it will be much easier and quicker to find exactly what you need. The last thing you want to be doing is pulling out stuff and searching through everything in an emergency. It's so important to keep the area clean, clear and with everything in its place.

### Getting started

To declutter and organise your medicine cupboard, follow my foolproof method set out in easy steps:

1.  Take everything out of the cupboard and divide it into categories, such as pharmacy (medications, cough mixture, pain-relief capsules, etc.); bandages, gauze, dressings and

69

plasters; creams and ointments; itch and allergy potions; outdoor products (lip salves and sun lotion); and first-aid items.

2. Sort through each category and purge. Just like food that's past its sell-by date, expired medications can become ineffective or even toxic. We all hang on to them, but the time has come to get rid of anything that's out of date. Once you have a pile of expired prescribed medication, simply pop it down to your local pharmacy. The staff there will dispose of it safely.

3. Decide how you want to organise the contents of the cupboard. A lot depends on quantity. If you don't have many items, you could use two lidded containers – one for adults and the other for children. However, if you have a lot of medications and first-aid equipment, it's best to store them in labelled clear plastic containers. This makes it easier to identify what's what in an emergency, as well as when you have run out of something and need to replace it.

4. Think about where you are going to locate your medicine cupboard. You need easy access, but it must also be out of the way of young children and not at floor level. Use containers with tightly fitting lids to prevent items falling out.

Never waste an opportunity. For instance, while you're waiting for the bath to fill up, give the sink and toilet a quick clean. Or when you've applied a facemask and you're waiting for it to dry, give the mirrors and taps a quick polish. To help with this, keep a small box of cleaning products handy in the cupboard under the sink or the linen cupboard. If it's nearby, you'll be more inclined to keep things clean on a regular basis and it won't seem like a dreaded task.

## Creating the right mood

Last but not least, think about how you can lend an air of serenity to your bathroom, giving it that soothing home-spa feel. A beautiful orchid, an aromatherapy candle, jars of pretty bath salts or some neatly rolled colourful bath towels will add the finishing touches and create an inviting space where you can relax.

**TGCO Top Tip** To keep your bathroom smelling fresh and clean, add a few drops of lavender essential oil to a cup of bicarbonate of soda and place it behind the toilet. You could also sprinkle a few drops inside the cardboard centre of the toilet paper roll. Essential oils are natural and, unlike many chemically based fragrances, they won't harm you.

## Bathroom to-do list

- Keep the sink, toilet, bath and shower clean. Encourage family members to wipe around the bath, basin and shower after using them.
- Use essential oils, candles or fragrant flowers to make it smell fresh and welcoming.
- Open the windows for a little while each day to air the room.
- Don't leave wet towels lying on the floor – hang them up to dry. Do the same with wet bath mats.
- Keep a container of cleaning products in the cupboard or under the sink for easy access.
- Make sure you go through your make-up and medicines regularly, so that you're not holding on to expired items.

# Declutter Your Kitchen

My favourite room in the house is the kitchen. It's the heart of my home where everyone congregates and comes together as a family and it's where the magic happens! But this important space can quickly get overrun with all sorts of stuff, like cooking utensils, gadgets, food, recipe books, cleaning products and children's toys. Imposing a structure on this area will make you feel wonderfully calm and bring you satisfaction every time you use it.

## Getting started

A kitchen, especially a large one, can seem like an overwhelming challenge when you decide to declutter it. But remember, it's OK to *not* do it all. So before you get going and pull everything out of the cupboards, TGCO recommends you write a plan with some clearly defined goals to make the task ahead less daunting and help you feel more in control of the whole process:

- Look at your storage areas and how many cabinets and drawers you have. Do you use everything that's inside them?
- Think about which areas you use for specific tasks. Are you making the most of them?
- Make a list of what you need to do for each zone and then tick off the jobs as you go along.

# Dividing your kitchen into zones

For many of us the kitchen is the most important room in the house, but have you organised this space to make it work for you? A kitchen functions best when it's set up in the following zones:

- Prep area
- Larder and food storage
- Cooking utensils
- Serving ware
- Entertaining ware
- Seasonal ware
- Cleaning cupboard
- Dining space (if you have one)

Everything in your kitchen should fit into one of these zones.

# Step by step ...

Decide which areas need the most organising and whether you are in the mood to start with them or leave them to last, focusing on the easier zones first. As always, the TGCO principles apply. You need to declutter first then clean and organise afterwards:

1. Collect all the items in one zone or area and sort them into categories.
2. Go through the items in each pile and decide which you want to keep and which you want to rehome or bin.
3. Clean the area where you plan to store them.
4. Put them away in a neat, tidy and organised way.
5. You can feel good about what you've achieved, so treat yourself to a cup of tea and a biscuit or whatever else you fancy, then move on to the next task.

*What makes a kitchen great is not always its size or space, but how you use it.*

## Storage solutions

We all have so much stuff in our kitchen that storage space can be a big issue. A well-planned kitchen will have plenty of storage with all the utensils, tools and appliances we need close to hand and in the right place. As we accumulate more gadgets and machines, though, and the cupboards fill up with more mugs and glasses and the drawers with additional knives and cutlery, things can start to get out of control. But don't panic – TGCO is on hand to help you make the best use of the available space and to organise it efficiently and neatly. And remember, storage solutions don't have to be boring; think outside the box (!) and let your creative juices flow.

**TGCO Top Tip**

If space is at a premium in your kitchen, you can affix self-adhesive hooks inside cabinet doors for hanging utensils and tea towels, etc. Or you can mount a kitchen-roll holder or foil dispenser, to save space elsewhere.

## Kitchen cupboards

We all have so many cupboards in our kitchens that it can be a bit overwhelming. Make sure you keep your storage and food cupboards separate, as this will make it a lot easier to stay organised.

### *Food cupboards*

Do you struggle to keep your food organised? If so, don't worry – you're not alone. Follow my practical ideas and tips and you'll be showing off the inside of your cupboards to everyone who walks into your kitchen.

Start by dividing your food cupboards into zones. This will not only keep your foodstuffs organised, but also make prepping quicker and easier, as you won't spend so much time looking for things. And when you write your weekly shopping list it will be easier to stay on top of what you *need*, therefore keeping costs down.

1. Identify the food and cooking categories that suit your lifestyle, e.g. weeknight suppers, packed lunches, baking, etc.
2. Designate an area for each category with the most often-used zones within easy reach. If you don't have the space, use cupboard organisers to help – this will prevent waste, as everything will be visible inside.

The TGCO favourite storage solution for food cupboards is simple: clear rectangular containers. They are excellent for storing rice, pasta, cereals, beans and pulses. Cardboard boxes can clutter up your cupboards and take up a lot of room, *plus* you can't tell when they are nearly empty. On the other hand, clear containers help you stay more organised and look amazing. You can add labels to help identify what's inside and even cut the expiry date off the packet and stick it to the back of the container. Stack them neatly and you'll see at a glance where everything is and what needs replenishing.

You can use a lazy Susan to organise your herbs and spices, cooking oils and sauces. You'll find these items faster by simply rotating the base, and it will give greater depth to the cupboard, so you'll end up using them more.

It's a good idea to declutter your food cupboards once every three months, removing any out-of-date jars and cans and replacing them if needed.

**TGCO Top Tip** Using shelf risers and organisers will give your cupboard twice as much storage space. You can even buy folding shelves that fit inside your cupboards to create extra space.

# Clean Out Your Spices and Herbs

Does your heart sink when you open a cupboard and there are half-used bottles, jars and packets of spices and herbs shoved inside in no particular order, often balancing on top of each other? If so, the time has come to sort, purge and organise them:

1. Put them all on the kitchen table where you can see them.
2. Discard any that are past their expiry date – they will have lost their intensity of flavour.

3. Check for duplicates. There's a good chance you'll have two or three jars of cinnamon or mixed herbs. Chuck any that are nearly empty.
4. Place the spices and herbs in clear stacking containers that take up less space and contain them neatly.
5. Make sure your jars are clearly labelled and place them in alphabetical order, so you can see at a glance what they are. This will make your life so much easier.

**TGCO Top Tip** Whether you have plastic or glass food-storage containers, TGCO recommends separating the lids and popping them neatly into their own container, while stacking the containers themselves on top of each other.

### *Storage cupboards*

What I've discovered in my work, as well as in my own home, is that owning less is better than organising more, and this is particularly apt when sorting out kitchen storage cupboards. We all have so many mugs, beakers, glasses, flasks and water bottles, but rarely use them all, just sticking to our tried-and-trusted favourites. You need to be really ruthless when decluttering these, only keeping the items you use and donating those you don't. Then place the ones you do use inside special trays or containers to prevent them falling over and enabling you to select them with ease. That way you get to use everything inside the cupboard and not just whatever is at the front. Make sure you're careful when removing things, though – the container will be heavy.

*Owning less is better than organising more.*

## Mugs and cups

These deserve a special mention because we all accumulate too many, and however much you love your morning or afternoon cuppa, you don't need shelves and shelves of mugs and cups, often stacked inside each other just to fit them in. If opening this cupboard is like a scene from a crowded commuter train, it's time to declutter.

1. Have a count of your mugs and cups and ask yourself whether you really need that number between you.
2. Empty the shelves and put everything on the worktop.
3. Clean the cupboard, giving it a good wipe over.
4. Now it's time to get tough and sort through the mugs and cups. Be ruthless yet mindful. Everything you throw away will end up in landfill, so always recycle/donate where possible. By donating your surplus mugs to local charity shops, schools, nursing homes and shelters, you'll be supporting people in need.
5. Return the mugs and cups to the cupboard, replacing them neatly, or hang them from hooks below the overhead cupboards and above the worktop. You can also display the attractive ones on open shelves or mug trees.

## China and glass

As always, try to keep only what you're going to use and avoid filling your kitchen with occasional-entertaining china and glassware. Organise crockery by type: so, dinner plates on their own, then side plates and bowls. And when it comes to glasses it makes sense to arrange by style and then size.

### *Pots and pans*

For pots and pans, TGCO likes to store the lids in vertical slotted organisers and stack the pans on top. Alternatively, if space is at a premium, you can hang them from a rack attached to the wall or from a circular or square hanging rack suspended over your island, if you have one. If you select this option, you'll need a high ceiling, otherwise the pans can get in the way and block your view.

If you have a standard hob with four or five rings, you don't need more than six pans, so keep it simple and stick to what you use. As long as you have a large, medium and small saucepan, a non-stick pan, a frying pan and griddle pan, you'll have the basics. (Of course, enthusiastic home cooks may also have a wok, an omelette pan, a sauté pan, a preserving pan, etc.) If you don't have the space to store all your pans in a drawer under the oven or in cupboards and shelving units, and you can't bear to part with them, you will have to consider other solutions, such as hanging them from racks, rails and curtain poles.

## Drawers

For me, happiness is a clean, tidy and organised drawer. There are few things worse than pulling open a drawer and everything inside is in a mess and you can't see what you want. And there's no excuse when there are so many great drawer organisers and inserts available. Here are some options for organising your drawers so they stay neat and tidy:

- **Drawer dividers** will prevent items from moving around inside the drawer.
- **Drawer organisers and inserts** can be purchased in stay-put, expanding or interlocking formats to fit any size of drawer.

## *Utensils drawers*

This is often the worst drawer in the kitchen, so full of stuff shoved in and piled up haphazardly that it's impossible to find what you want without emptying it all out. And, believe me, there's nothing more irritating and frustrating when you're in the middle of cooking the family's supper or having a Sunday-afternoon baking session.

1.  Empty the drawer and sort the items into the following categories:
    *   **Everyday items:** can opener, garlic press, peeler, masher, grater, whisk, apple corer, oven thermometer, meat baster.
    *   **Cooking utensils:** wooden spoons, slicers, stirrers, sieve.
    *   **Cutting tools:** kitchen knives, cheese knife, scissors, poultry shears.
    *   **Measuring and baking:** measuring spoons, pastry brush, rolling pin, cookie cutters.
2.  The drawer needs to be clean and clear, so think about which items you use and would work back inside the drawer. Purge any you don't use.
3.  Clean the drawer thoroughly and, if you don't already have one, place an expandable drawer insert or organiser inside before filling with the items you want to keep.

**Caution!** Take special care with knives. It's so easy to cut yourself. Use a special in-drawer knife organiser, knife protector or chef's roll.

## *Cutlery drawers*

Most of us have far too much cutlery clogging up our kitchen drawers. It tends to accumulate over the years as you buy more sets, are given a canteen as a present or relatives and friends donate items.

One thing I have learned is that you can never have enough teaspoons, and, like socks, they have a habit of mysteriously disappearing, so there's no need to cull your collection of these ruthlessly. However, you really don't need in excess of 20 knives, forks and soup/dessertspoons, unless you throw lots of parties for huge numbers of guests. For the average family of four, a set of, say, six or eight of each cutlery item used daily is enough. If you have a special set for entertaining, store it separately or keep it in a purpose-made cutlery canteen. Donate the cutlery you don't want to keep to local charity shops and shelters which will make good use of them.

### Junk drawers

The main reason why these exist is to catch the things that don't really have a home. Your junk drawer is not like your other kitchen drawers where you tuck away the same eight forks, knives and spoons in neatly designated areas. It needs to hold all manner of things from batteries, string and tape measures to pens, note pads and keys. It's no wonder that it's often such a mess, with everything crammed in at random.

1.  Empty out all the contents and think about which items are really useful.
2.  Purge what you don't want or need and sort the remaining items into separate piles.
3.  Now your 'junk' is organised don't just shove it back in the drawer, so the vicious circle starts all over again. Instead, invest in a special drawer insert, gadget organiser (they come in a variety of colours and sizes) or a set of dividers to separate the different categories and enable you to keep everything neat and tidy. This will give your items space, so you can see at a glance what you've got and go straight to whatever it is you need.
4.  Alternatively, reuse some household items such as clean takeaway plastic containers, clear ice-cream tubs, clear glass candle jars and shallow plastic storage containers that have lost their lids.

## Under the sink

I love cleaning under the kitchen sink because it's often the most forgotten area in the house. For many of us, finding storage space here is often tricky thanks to water softeners, waste disposals and, of course, pipework, and this area is a chaotic mess. So, it's important to use every inch of available space wisely to store your go-to cleaning supplies. I like to use under-the-sink organisers and containers. They allow you to store cleaning products, sponges and accessories neatly, so you can access them easily and see what's there to prevent duplication in your weekly shop. Some of them also help you to reclaim space height-wise, effectively adding an extra shelf.

As usual, you need to pull everything out, purge and organise. After you've emptied the cupboard, clean it thoroughly before replacing items in their relevant categories in clear or low-level containers. You could sort them into, say, general household, dishwasher, washing and kitchen supplies. This will prevent you from accumulating eight bottles of kitchen spray and 25 sponges.

**Caution!** If you have young children and/or pets, be sure to fit a child safety-lock device to the cupboard door. Some of the cleaning products inside may well be toxic.

To keep your kitchen sink clean and bacteria-free you can make your own DIY sink cleaner. Mix equal parts of white vinegar and warm water in a spray bottle and give it a good shake. Then simply spray your sink and leave for a few minutes before wiping it down with a clean cloth. Hurrah! You now have a clean and fresh sink.

## The fridge

I clean and declutter my fridge once every two weeks, so I can keep on top of what's inside. And I always feel fantastic afterwards. If you don't make time for this task, it's all too likely that you'll find some unpleasant items lurking at the back – the smell will be a tell-tale sign.

1.  Start off by removing all the contents of the fridge and placing them on the kitchen table or worktop.
2.  Next, remove the drawers and shelves and clean them either with some warm, mild soapy water or my white vinegar and warm water mixture (see box above). This will disinfect them and neutralise any smells.
3.  When they are dry, replace them and then you can start organising. Go through all the fresh products with a limited shelf life, such as dairy, and dispose of any that are past their sell-by dates or starting to smell. Be especially careful with meat, fish and poultry. Check any jars and don't bother keeping those that are gungy at the bottom or have only a spoonful left inside.
4.  Sort out the fruit and vegetables, removing any that are bruised, smelly or soft and past their best.

5. Now replace the food in its designated space. I like to use containers wherever possible, especially in the fruit and vegetable drawers.

**TGCO Top Tip**

Want to organise your fridge without spending any money? Why not reuse your fruit and vegetable plastic cartons as storage containers? Simply clean them in warm, soapy water, dry and place inside your fridge. Not only do they look great, this also prevents them going to landfill and they do an excellent job of keeping everything in their place.

# Kitchen to-do list

- Empty the bins every day to avoid old food smells.
- Load the dishwasher throughout the day and turn it on at the end of the evening, so everything is sparkling clean and it's ready to empty first thing the following morning.
- Spray and clean your worktops every day.
- Clean the sink once a day to prevent a build-up of bacteria.
- Clean your kitchen floor at least twice a week, more often if you have pets or young children.
- Give everything in the kitchen a good clean at least once a week.
- Clean and tidy your fridge every two weeks.
- Clean out and tidy drawers and cupboards once every two or three months.

*It's OK to not do it all.*

# Declutter Your Living Space

The living space, or family room, is where the whole family can chill out, chat, watch television, play games and read. For me, it's a peaceful place where we can enjoy each other's company and make memories together.

I think it's important to maximise your living room's functionality, while containing your clutter, which can quickly creep up on you, so that before you know it you have a full-blown disaster. By planning and designating specific imaginative go-to areas for different activities and putting the TGCO decluttering plan into action, you can keep your living space relaxing and tidy.

## Getting started

Go into your living room and take a long, hard look at it. How large is it and are you making the best use of the available space? What do you want to use it for? Think about the layout and how you could create different areas within it. You might consider some of the following:

- A sitting area
- A reading area
- A TV/home cinema area
- A music area
- A play area
- A storage area for DVDs, CDs, books, magazines, games

# Make it cosy

Keep the sitting and lounging area snug and cosy, so you'll feel good when you sit down and put your feet up after a hard day's work. Some soft lighting, colourful soft cushions, stunning holders for your scented candles and a vase of flowers or an attractive pot plant will all help to create the right atmosphere and make you feel relaxed. It's so easy and needn't cost a fortune. Sometimes rearranging the furniture can make a big difference to the ambience of the room too and make the best use of the space available. Try it and see. It's also a great workout!

## Storage solutions

To keep your living room looking neat and clutter-free you'll need some smart storage solutions, such as cupboards, stacking systems, shelving and tidiers. Of course, rather than having one designated area for everything, you could separate different items: so, you could keep all your books on a shelving system in the reading area if you have one, the DVDs could be close to the television and the CDs or vinyl records (if you still have any) near the music system. There are no set rules and whatever works for you is best.

### Books

We all seem to end up with too many books and not enough room. If your books are sitting in piles on the floor or your shelves are bowing under their weight, you need to declutter.

Only keep the books you need for reference and those you love and enjoy reading. I've always applied the 'one-in-and-one-out' rule with books coming into our house. This allows you to manage the clutter in this area and doesn't cause problems when it comes to storing them. You can donate the books you don't want any more to charity shops or even your local library.

I like to keep all my books in one place, so my cookbooks, fiction and non-fiction are all in my living room. You can organise your library by author in alphabetical order, by genre (e.g. cookery, gardening, history, thrillers, sci-fi, etc.). Some people even choose to do it by colour, although it can be very time-consuming looking for that book you need if you can't remember the colour of the spine!

## CDs and DVDs

Are you or your partner still living in a world full of DVDs and CDs? I have to admit that we still have quite a large collection, mainly because my husband loves them and can't bear to part with them. However, as we all know, nowadays most movies and music are streamed online or can be downloaded on demand. This not only makes them more accessible and immediate, but it's also great when it comes to reducing the clutter in your home.

If your collection has got to the stage where it needs sorting, culling and organising, set aside a quiet hour or two for decluttering. As always, go through everything, sorting it into categories. Keep what you enjoy or want to watch or listen to again and put the rest aside in a separate pile for recycling or selling. There's a hungry market for second-hand CDs (especially audio books) and DVDs and it's simple to sell them online or at car-boot sales. If you don't have the time to sell them, why not donate them to your local hospital where patients might be able to benefit from them? And how about local retirement communities and nursing homes? Movie nights and music will brighten up the residents' days. Audio books are great for visually sighted and blind people.

Next, classify what you want to keep by genre, alphabetically, or even by colour (although, again, this may slow you down if you're going through your whole collection looking for something specific). It's a good idea to organise all your box sets together in a separate container. Special storage folders are a fabulous solution for freeing up bookshelves and cupboards, which are often overflowing with DVDs and CDs. However, if they are not in their correct covers or labelled or displayed properly, you will forget what's inside. TGCO recommends placing your discs inside the sleeves along with the front cover of the film or album, making this a go-to organised solution.

## Magazines

If you subscribe to a favourite periodical, purchase a newspaper every day or the fat Sunday editions with the colour supplements, or you just can't resist the inviting covers on display at the supermarket checkout, it won't be long before you start to feel overrun.

TGCO recommends that you declutter and organise magazines at least once a month to keep on top of things. As always, sort them into categories, decide what you want to keep and put what you don't want into the recycling bin. Just keep the latest editions out on display, close at hand, and if there are too many of the older ones to store in neat piles on the coffee table, use a magazine rack or holder. There are so many types to choose from and they come in a variety of colours to suit your décor.

# Play areas

Not many of us have the space or the luxury of a specially designated children's playroom at home, but for those who do, it
doesn't take more than a couple of days for this to fill up with
toys and mess and to get out of control. Likewise, an open-plan
living space that acts as a family area, dining room and playroom
can quickly become overwhelmed by clutter, too, and resemble
more of a kids' soft-play area than a family home.

By introducing baskets or neat stacking storage boxes you
can store the toys in category order. This will give them a home,
plus it will create 'go-to' areas for the children. Small items, such
as Lego, building blocks, paint, crayons and pens, should be
boxed up in labelled clear containers. Your living space is meant
to be functional and to work for everyone, while allowing your
little darlings to use their imagination and creativity to play and
explore. Establish some ground rules and encourage your
children to tidy up after they've finished playing (see p. 56). If
clearing up becomes a familiar part of their everyday routine,
rather than an unpleasant chore, they won't throw a hissy fit and
will go into auto-pilot mode.

# Slime

Love it or hate it, it's here and our kids are either making it, buying it or watching other people make it online, while we cringe at the thought of it coming into our homes.

My youngest daughter is obsessed with the revolting stuff – but when she plays with it, she's happy, content and in full-on creative mode. Still, I got fed up with seeing my kitchen spoons, bowls and containers being used and stored in the play area. So, something had to be done and *fast*. I've created an organised slime station: one that contains the slime ingredients, mixing bowls and spoons, plus the dreaded slime itself. I wanted something that could be wheeled out of the room when necessary, but which would also complement our décor. Luckily, I managed to source a great trolley that works a treat.

**TGCO Top Tip**

If the kids happen to drop slime on the carpet, mix up the following solution: two-thirds white vinegar to one-third warm water. Use a soft brush to loosen the slime, then a clean, dry towel to blot it dry. If it doesn't all come out the first time, repeat the process.

# Underst: space

If you have stairs in your living room leading up to the floor above, you may well have some room beneath them. Designed well, this triangular portion of space can become a handy extra storage area within your home.

## Understairs cupboard

If your understairs space is a cupboard, with angled proportions, it's probably cluttered and full of all the junk and stuff that gets shoved in because you don't know where else to hide it. More often than not, it's only the things at the very front that ever get to see the light of day. If so, it's time to think about what you want to store inside and the best and most space-efficient way of doing so.

1.  Start by pulling out every last item and then thoroughly clean, dust and vacuum the space.
2.  Sort through the clutter, scrutinising, discarding or relocating it. If you have cans of paint or sports equipment, perhaps they would be better stored in the garage, if you have one, leaving the understairs area free for everyday items like shopping bags, dog leads and shoes.
3.  Before you put back the remaining items, think about the space and how you can make it work for you. Perhaps you could fit shelves or cupboards to make it neater, or you may even consider redesigning it. Just be mindful and, whatever you decide to do, keep all similar items together and in one place.

**An open understairs area**

If your understairs area is open and you've perhaps always considered it to be 'a waste of space', well, think again – it may have potential. If so, embrace it. This dull, nondescript area could be transformed into a snug, a mini office area or even your very own bar.

## Living room to-do list

- Fluff up your cushions every day, so that your sofa is inviting. It will help make the whole room look tidier too.
- Make the room cosy with some candles, blankets or plants – it can make all the difference.
- Invest in smart storage solutions that work for your home and your routine.
- Make sure everything has its place and organise it all in a way that means you can find things again.

# Declutter Your Study/ Home Office

If you work from home, you'll understand how important it is to love your work space. This is the dedicated room or area where you house your computer, store your files, communicate with your clients, keep track of your accounts and manage your household accounts and correspondence. Working in this space will be pleasant and productive if it's neat, tidy and organised, but if it's full of clutter and your heart sinks when you step inside, you could find yourself getting into a mess in more ways than one. So, it's time to sort it out, declutter and put the TGCO Decluttering Plan into action.

# Getting started

1. Start the decluttering process by removing everything from the room apart from the furniture you wish to keep.
2. Sort through the contents and arrange them into four piles:
   - Keep
   - Donate
   - Bin (or shred)
   - Sell
3. File away the paperwork you want to keep in a filing cabinet. It's a great way to free up space in your home office. Buying a lockable fireproof cabinet ensures that your important documents won't get stolen or destroyed.
4. Get rid of the paperwork you don't want to keep. A home shredder is so useful for disposing of confidential papers such as old bank statements, and the shreddings will take up less room in the recycling bin.
5. If you have a mass of wires and cables in your office, try to reduce the number of these by getting rid of any electronic equipment you no longer use. Investing in wireless devices will also reduce cable clutter and the remaining ones can be tied together so they stay in one place, out of your way. Route the wires through the hole in your desk, if you have one, and make sure they're all behind or below your desk or against a wall – away from open areas where someone might trip over them.

Creating a calm, enjoyable workspace is simpler and less taxing than it sounds. Start off by planning how you would like the space to work for you and then reconfigure your ideal layout.

Who says you have to put your desk against a wall or below a window? If you have a study, home office or studio, you could try placing it in the middle of the room to give the space more 'depth' and a focal point, making it less dull. This works particularly well in a small room, when you want to make it look bigger. There are no set rules, so be creative and don't be afraid to move things around and rearrange the furniture to make it more ergonomic and find out what works best for you.

## Storage solutions

Not everyone has a dedicated room for their home office – it might just be a corner in your living room, for example. No matter how much or how little space you have, however, your study area should not cause you undue stress.

My favourite way to organise this space is with shelving and pretty, labelled boxes. Floating shelves are a great option to add storage without taking up too much space. A bookcase could work well too. Try not to hoard pens; just keep a pot with the ones you need on your desk. I love to use a rainbow-coloured plastic organiser for my paperwork but if you prefer a filing cabinet, that's fine. It's all about what is best for you.

## Paperwork

Paperwork is often the most pressing issue, so why not tackle it first and get it out of the way? I don't know about you but the amount of paper that enters our home is nothing short of crazy. First, there's the daily post, then there's the letters inside the children's schoolbags and let's not forget the emails, online bank statements and web search results that we print out. And if that sounds a lot, it doesn't include receipts, takeaway menus, warranties, certificates, insurance documents, etc. It all accumulates so rapidly and keeps repeating itself … like Groundhog Day!

TGCO has some useful tips to help bring calm to this dreaded task.

1. Subscribe to Royal Mail's opt-out service to reduce the amount of unwanted mail you receive. It really does make a difference.

2. Assign a special place where you can put every family member's post each day, so they know where to look and nothing gets lost.

3. Open letters and bills and action them straight away. If you put them to one side, you're more likely to get distracted and forget about them. And by the time you get around to dealing with them, it may be too late.

4. Keep important documents – such as your passport, driver's licence, insurance documents, birth and marriage certificates, etc. – in a soft folder somewhere safe, such as a locked filing cabinet or drawer in your desk. By storing them all in one place, it's easy to access them quickly when you're in a hurry or in an emergency, such as a house fire or burst water pipe.

5. Sort out a filing arrangement that works for you. It could be a stacking system with drawers or containers for new mail, pending paperwork and all the stuff you've dealt with that you need to file away for safekeeping. Or you may prefer a traditional filing cabinet or soft folders.

**TGCO Top Tip**

Studying at home for an exam or course can be quite messy, with paperwork everywhere, so keep it simple and introduce a storage tower. TGCO recommends you organise each tray by topic or subject order and then simply label them. This system will keep your revision notes, paperwork and study material neat, tidy, organised and easily accessible ... plus you'll feel calmer and in control knowing where everything is.

**TGCO Top Tip**

I love memo/vision boards. I use them for my to-do lists, reminders, photos and pages I've cut out of magazines, etc. They motivate and inspire me to achieve my goals and play a vital role in my office. You can buy or make one yourself – there are lots of ideas online about how to go about it. I also like to use a magnetic, write-on or calendar-style board to record all of my important events each month.

# Your computer

There's nothing sexy about a cluttered inbox, especially when it's home to old messages, old concerns and old news. Just keeping up with your inbox sometimes feels like a full-time job, so here are some TGCO tips to help you cut down the time you spend dealing with emails and allow you to concentrate on other important tasks – like finishing the next level of Candy Crush …

- **Don't mix personal and business emails.** Maintain a clear distinction between your work and personal accounts. You are more likely to be distracted and open emails from family members and friends during work hours, so keep them separate.
- **Remove yourself from unwanted email newsletters.** That way, the only emails you'll see in your inbox are ones that you can either read or quickly dismiss. It may take a couple of evenings and a few weeks to remove them as they come in, but I highly recommend it.
- **Be wary of social media.** They can also generate a lot of unwanted emails. I recently signed up to LinkedIn. That's great, but I've started to receive a ton of emails telling me about who just updated their job or their experience and endorsements. Remember that you can turn off the email notifications from the settings. I did this on day three!
- **Introduce filters and folders.** Microsoft Outlook and Gmail allow you to structure emails in clever ways. In Outlook I have folders categorised into the relevant subjects, so that I can sort out my emails as quickly as possible. This helps keep my inbox empty.
- **Stay on top of things.** To wrap things up, just get into the habit of periodically checking, filing and deleting your mail and soon you'll achieve your email Utopia.

**TGCO Top Tip**

Love them or hate them, emails won't disappear until you do something about it: read your email > reply **OR** unsubscribe **OR** file in your folders **OR** delete. It's as simple as that!

## Study/home office to-do list

- Create a calm, enjoyable workspace for yourself. Maybe move furniture around to inject new life into the room.
- File away your paperwork to make space. The room will immediately feel better once the piles are cleared.
- Sort out your devices. It's all very well working in a tidy office, but you don't want to open your computer and be bombarded by thousands of unread emails. You can tackle this step by step to make it less overwhelming.
- Set up a memo/vision board. You won't believe how motivating and uplifting these can be.

# Declutter Your Laundry/ Utility Room

Sundays are generally the day we choose to rest, catch up with family and friends, prep for the week ahead and, for some of us at least, do the week's laundry. By decluttering and organising your laundry area or utility room, laundry will be less of a chore and you might even feel encouraged to do that little bit more every other day. Here are some TGCO tips to inspire you.

## Getting started

Start off by getting some laundry baskets. I like to use three medium-sized baskets for separating darks, whites and colours, plus one smaller one for wool and delicate items. I label each one clearly, so everyone in the family can see where to put their dirty laundry. No excuses.

Declutter your laundry room and make sure you're not hoarding unnecessary cleaning products or keeping items in there that don't belong. Take everything out of the cupboards and then make an inventory, so you don't buy things you don't need.

**TGCO Top Tip**

Missing and odd socks can be a real pain during the laundry process. To prevent this happening, I peg small fabric washing bags or pillowcases to a linen basket. I then add the dirty socks and delicate underwear to the bags, and once they are full, I wash them separately, empty them to dry the contents and then organise them when I put them back in the underwear drawers.

## Storage solutions

If you have the space, then functional shelving is a great way to keep your laundry area tidy.

I love using labelled baskets so that my family know where everything belongs. They're also great for hiding the clean clothes that you haven't got around to sorting out yet.

As elsewhere, use clear containers to house your laundry cleaning products. These enable you to see what you have and what needs replacing when you do your weekly shopping list, and also keep everything neatly in one place.

## Avoiding laundry breakdowns

The laundry room is often one of the most disorganised and cluttered spaces in our homes. Everything gets dumped there and then we shut the door to hide the mess or pretend to ourselves that it doesn't exist. Do you spend valuable time during the week collecting random items of dirty laundry from around the house, then dumping them in the basket and doing your best to forget they exist until the weekend comes around? Well, rest assured, there are some simple measures you can take to get organised and prevent further laundry breakdowns.

- **Washing a load of laundry every day or as soon as the basket is full** will mean that you need *fewer* clothes. FACT! You don't really need 25 pairs of socks or 40 pairs of knickers if you follow this simple procedure because only a couple of pairs will be in the laundry system at any one time.
- **If you're busy with a demanding job** and don't work from home, wash your laundry in the evening before going to bed. First thing the following morning, simply hang it out to dry and air, then go about your day. Then, when you get back home in the evening, just fold it and put it away in its designated place. Simple.

Now all that's left to do is to crack open the vino and sit on the sofa with a big, smug smile on your face.

# Linen and towels

Linen and towel cupboards are, for many people, one of their least favourite areas to organise. There's a lot of folding involved, you can never find what you want when you want it, and you risk everything toppling on top of you every time you pull out a hand towel. However, if you struggle to keep your cupboard clear and organised, don't worry. TGCO has advice and tips that will prevent any more linen-cupboard disasters.

## Getting started

Ideally, all your linen and towels should be readily visible for everyone in the house.

1.  The best way to start is to take a good look at the space available and to determine what works and what doesn't.
2.  Now empty the cupboard, removing everything from the shelves. This is a really important part of the subtraction process. When our basic assumption is that we're just getting rid of a few items here and there, there's a tendency not to subtract enough.
3.  Now you can review all the towels, bed linen and blankets and start sorting and purging them. Be ruthless: do you really need 30 bath towels for four of you? Discard those that have had their day or that you no longer use. (As a guide, I keep four bath towels, four hand towels and four flannels per person, but you must do whatever works for you.) Towels don't stay soft and fluffy forever and most of us hang on to them long after they start to feel rough and scratchy. Throw these out or recycle them for use as towels for your pets if you have any. **Note:** you can donate old, clean towels, linen and blankets to homeless or dog shelters, which are always grateful to receive them (see p. 192).
4.  Clean the shelves and get ready to put back what you use in logical 'zones', grouping items together, so it makes functional sense. For instance, you can neatly fold or roll all the large towels, the hand towels, the bath mats and face flannels and put them on separate shelves or in colour-coordinated groups.
5.  When it comes to bed linen, I only keep two sets of sheets per bed. I neatly fold the set of duvet, fitted sheet and three pillow cases and place them inside a matching pillowcase. This method keeps everything together and makes life much easier when it comes to finding the exact set you're looking for. Making beds has never been so joyous.

TGCO
Top Tip
There are many ways of folding your towels, but I like to roll mine and keep them consistent throughout the cupboard. It's easy on the eye, it saves space and everyone in the house can do it.

## Storage solutions

I like to use dedicated baskets and containers for my linen and towels, especially items that are hard to stack neatly, such as flannels. They keep them tidy, stopping them toppling over into disarray. Line them up and designate what you'd like to go inside each one.

If you want the rest of your family on board with maintaining your new organised space, you'll need to make it easy for them. I find it useful to label the containers, just so everyone else knows where to find things and can easily put items away by themselves. Don't assume that they'll put the towels back in the 'right' spot if they don't know where that is. Another easy solution is to label the shelves.

# Laundry/utility room to-do list

- Try to do laundry as often as you can to avoid a breakdown. It doesn't take that long and you'll be amazed at the difference it can make.
- You could get a laundry basket that encourages separating lights from darks, so you don't even have to worry about sorting them before washing.

- Find storage solutions for your linens and towels that work for you and revisit them every so often to make sure they don't need replacing.
- Try to fold and put away clothes as soon as possible to stop clean items from building up. You'll quickly realise that you don't actually need 25 pairs of socks.

# Declutter Your Entrance Room/Hall

The entrance to your home is important because it's the first thing your visitors see when they enter. Yet it can often be neglected and overlooked – a magnet for clutter. First impressions count, so it's important to give this spot some TLC, making it an inviting space to welcome you home, too.

I always remember how much my nan used to love sweeping her steps and cleaning and polishing the front door and entrance every day. She took real pride in presenting this area as neat, organised and welcoming. Life is super-busy, and even I don't have the time to do this on a daily basis, but if you can declutter, clean and tidy your entrance space bi-weekly, it will be easier to manage it in a calm and organised way.

## Getting started

As usual, empty all the items in the room before sorting them into those you are going to keep and those that will be donated or binned. Think about how you are going to store the things you need or love. There are many ways to add value to this space to make it not only more functional, but also more welcoming and pleasing on the eye.

1. Hang some paintings or set a bowl or vase of colourful flowers on the hall table, if you have one. Your entrance will feel more spacious and open with an eye-catching wall mirror to reflect the light. Look at the lighting too. Is it warm and inviting, or too harsh, too dark or too bright?
2. Coats and shoes tend to multiply if you don't pay regular attention to them. Make sure you revisit these every so often, so they don't pile up – only those that are used every day should stay by the door. Put some coat hooks on the wall to free up floor space or use a free-standing coat stand.
3. Why not introduce a bench? This would allow you to sit down and remove your shoes, especially if they are dirty, dusty or muddy, before walking further into the house.
4. Keep additional clutter out of sight with a console table that has divided drawers to store the essentials, such as car keys and loose change.
5. Introduce some fragrance to make your entrance smell inviting. A vase of flowers, a reed diffuser or some pot pourri sprinkled with essential oils will divert attention from any unwelcoming smells from nearby shoes, as well as creating that pleasant, fresh aroma whenever you walk into your home.

*Your entrance hall will feel more spacious and open with an eye-catching wall mirror to reflect the light.*

## Storage solutions

I love clever, concealed storage in entrance halls. Some attractive, labelled wicker or reed storage baskets will make it easy to find exactly what you're looking for.

TGCO recommends that you use a colour-coded basket to keep shoes neat and organised. But make sure they're deep enough to contain everyone's shoes. Floating shelves are another option – they're easy to install and do not take up valuable floor space.

If you do invest in a bench, try to find one with storage underneath. This will be a win-win for tidying away items like wellies, umbrellas and pet accessories.

TGCO
Top Tip

A bulletin board by the entrance will grab the attention of everyone passing through; use it to display Post-It notes, mail or even kids' artwork.

## Entrance room/hall to-do list

- Have designated spaces for shoes, coats and additional clutter (keys, loose change).
- Create a warm and inviting space that immediately relaxes you when you get home. Plants, pot pourri and a mirror can really help.
- Make sure your whole family knows where things go and where to find them. This will prevent the area from becoming cluttered again.

# Declutter Your Garage/ Garden Shed

Is your garage full to overflowing with children's toys, a spare fridge or freezer, clothes and items ready to take to car-boot sales, memory boxes, opened or empty paint cans, gardening and DIY tools, car accessories, cleaning materials and even paperwork? And that's not counting the bicycles, lawn mower and garden hoses. Let's face it: the garage and/or garden shed quickly and effortlessly fill up with piles of clutter – all the stuff that we don't want inside the house. And what's more, half the time it's stuff that doesn't even necessarily belong to us, items we never use or things we haven't got around to throwing out. I believe that the garage should be treated like any other room in the house. Everything inside it should have a place, be useful and serve a purpose. And anything that doesn't fit into these categories can be disposed of.

Now garages and sheds come in so many shapes and sizes, so before you start decluttering, have a think about what you really want to store inside yours and how you'd like them to look. Decide which items you use more than others and the categories they fall into. Then you can work out the types of zone you need to create and make a plan of the area. TGCO has some ideas to help you get organised and come up with storage solutions without tearing your hair out.

# Getting started

1.  Call your local council or charity shops in advance and arrange for a collection at the end of the decluttering day. That way, all your items can be taken away from your drive or front garden.
2.  Get some cardboard boxes from your local supermarket to help you categorise what you keep.
3.  Sort things out, one area at a time, removing everything. If you use this method, you will be able to keep, donate or bin items more effectively.
4.  When you've cleared out the garage or shed and it's empty, give it a thorough clean and sweep the floor. It's not like you can do this every week, so this is a good opportunity to get rid of dead bugs, cobwebs and whatever else may be lurking in this space.
5.  Install your shelving and hooks and hang up the things you use every day or regularly. Start replacing all your contained items in their designated zones. Pack away seasonal stuff and bulky items such as gym equipment and sport bags.
6.  Now, give yourself a pat on the back and make yourself a nice cup of tea or a glass of wine. You should feel euphoric when you see the results of all your hard work and gaze at your neat and tidy garage or shed. Just think how wonderful it is to be able to see and access all the items inside your newly organised space.

# Storage solutions

*   **Hanging items** in a garage or shed will automatically give you more floor space, allowing you to move around freely and to use the area more effectively.

- **A secure vertical shelving system** will help to minimise clutter, give items a home, create clearly defined zones within the space and, best of all, enable you to use the full height of the wall areas. It's also great for storing containers. I like to use a variety of sizes to contain items like light bulbs, batteries, paints, tools and picnic ware. It really does make your life easier and looking for things less stressful.

- **Utilise the ceiling** and fit some utility hooks so you can store items like ladders, kids' scooters and Christmas trees in a safe and secure manner.

- **Clear shoeboxes** are a great way to store handy items like tools, gloves and garden twine. It's all about seeing what you want to use.

- **Install a pegboard** to organise and display your tools. Again, if you can see them, you're more likely to use them. You can reuse washed-out jam or food jars to store items like nails and screws.

- **Label your containers** to prevent you from having to search endlessly for missing items. The garage and shed usually house all the things we seldom use. Putting a category name on the jar or box will make your forays into this area quicker, easier and less frustrating. You can use a label maker, chalkboard labels, hanging tags or vinyl stickers.

TGCO
Top Tip

Always keep a fire extinguisher in your garage or shed. It's home to many flammable and chemical products, so it's better to be safe than sorry.

# Garage/garden shed to-do list

- Once you have decluttered, make an inventory of everything in your garage/garden shed, so you know what is actually there. It's so easy to forget otherwise.
- Find the best storage solutions for you, so that you can find those Christmas decorations or that toolbox quickly and easily.
- Revisit it every so often to prevent clutter from building up.

So there you have it: TGCO's tips and tricks for creating an organised, clutter-free home. There is a lot of information in this chapter, so refer back to it as and when you need to. It might seem a bit overwhelming, and it's certainly not going to happen overnight – no one is expecting you to do this all in one go – but if you take it one step at a time, you'll soon have a wonderfully tidy home. Call up a friend or blast some music to make the process more enjoyable. And remember to make lots of lists to stay on track.

# *10 ways to . . .*
## clear your clutter

### 1.

**REMOVE EVERYTHING**

Lay out all of your items, so everything is visible. This is a vital step in the process because you'll see how much stuff you have and where you can start decluttering.

### 2.

**SORT IT OUT**

Place the items in four piles: keep; donate; bin; sell. This will make it easier when it comes to reviewing the items.

### 3.

**BE RUTHLESS**

Review your piles and let go of all the broken, old things and the stuff you don't use. It's taking up space in your home and you don't need it. You can use that space for things that make you smile.

### 4.

**CLEAN EVERYWHERE**

Remove all traces of dirt and dust from the area (see the next chapter for more on this).

# 5.

## STORE THINGS WELL

The best storage solutions are those that work for you and your routine. I've included lots of tips here, but spend time thinking about how you would like to access your items and what is most important in your house. What works for me might not work for you.

# 6.

## KEEP EVERYTHING ORGANISED

Once you've decided on your storage solutions, put everything away so that it is easy for you to find things. While colour-coordinated DVDs might look beautiful on a shelf, is that sustainable for you or will you spend hours looking for one DVD because you can't remember if it was blue or red?

# 7.

## USE AN INVENTORY

I like having an inventory for every room in my house. That way, I know what I own and where it is. This stops me from buying stuff that I already have.

# 8.

## DON'T FORGET ABOUT IT!

Once you've done your big declutter, make sure you keep on top of things. Taking 15 minutes once a month to organise your Tupperware, for example, will be much more sustainable than doing a giant kitchen clear-out once a year. Make lists, so that you know what to focus on when you go back to review.

# 9.

## REWARD YOURSELF

Make sure that once you've finished the job, you reward yourself. Thinking about enjoying a nice bubble bath in your clean and tidy bathroom will make it easier to keep going when you feel overwhelmed.

# 10.

## RELAX!

You don't have to be perfect. Life gets in the way and sometimes even my sheets go on my bed unironed. Don't sweat the small stuff and just do the best that you can.

# 3: Eco-cleaning

## Your Home

Lots of people don't like cleaning.
Don't get me wrong – I'm sure most of us
*love* a clean home, but spending lots
of energy on something you don't
particularly enjoy isn't the best pastime.
Like it or not, though, regular cleaning
is essential, and there are things you
can do to make the process speedier,
healthier and more eco-friendly.

I don't believe you have to spend hours cleaning your home – 30 minutes a day can work just fine. However, if you work full-time and are busy multi-tasking and juggling family commitments, childcare and a job, then it's important to work out a schedule that suits you, even if it's just once a week for a big top-to-bottom clean of the whole house. And if you can clean up in the kitchen after every meal and give the sink and shower a quick once over with some spray and a cloth after using them each day, the weekend cleaning session won't be such a chore.

# Natural Products

If you want to start cutting down on chemical cleaners and stop using single-use plastic cleaning bottles but have absolutely no idea how to go about it, then you've come to the right place. Read on and discover TGCO's smart solutions and useful tips on how to become an eco-warrior in your own home.

Whenever I walk down the cleaning-products aisle in a supermarket, I'm overwhelmed by the range of flammable and toxic cleaners. Some come with so many warnings that they scare the life out of me. Even many of the familiar household ones we've all used contain ingredients that are toxic, hazardous, non-biodegradable or derived from non-renewable resources like petroleum. And one thing they have in common is that they all have an adverse effect on the Earth's delicately balanced eco-systems. And don't get me started on plastic bottles: how many of these do you throw away? Did you know that it takes over 200 years for each spray bottle to decompose?

I'm just as careful about which cleaning products I use in my home as I am about what I put on my face or in my bath. After all, there's little point buying a natural organic bath oil if you pour it into a bath that's been cleaned with harsh chemicals. We're all becoming more environmentally conscious, embracing sustainability and shopping more ethically when it comes to food and cosmetics, so why not apply the same values to our homes? Your family will be healthier and happier if you swap cleaning products containing potentially toxic chemicals for more eco-friendly and natural ones.

I always advise having just a few multi-purpose natural products to take care of your general cleaning needs. We need to become more aware of the chemicals that are being released into the air we breathe, especially in our homes where we bring up our children. I started cutting down on chemical cleaners several years ago. Every time I cleaned the house I would cough and sneeze for hours afterwards, so I did some research and discovered that these were warning signs that my body didn't like being around these products. (And that's not to mention what they are doing to our waterways.) Cleaning products that contain VOCs (see box, p. 120) can contribute to higher pollution indoors than outdoors, so why not follow TGCO's example and make your home a greener and healthier place by making your own cleaning products or buying more natural eco-friendly versions of the ones you usually use. They're safer for you, your family, your home and the environment.

*There's little point buying a natural organic bath oil if you pour it into a bath that's been cleaned with harsh chemicals.*

# Reducing and avoiding VOCs

VOCs (volatile organic compounds) are found in many of the common household cleaning products we use. They release colourless gases into the air which linger long after use and, for some sensitive people, exposure can be associated with a host of health issues, ranging from liver and kidney damage to problems with the central nervous system. If possible, avoid paints, varnishes, cleaners and solvents that contain VOCs and make sure you do your research. One of the most important things to do is to keep your home well ventilated. Open the windows and let in the fresh air every day. You don't need a research study to tell you that something that's suspiciously bright blue or smells completely fake probably isn't that great for your health or the environment.

When I stopped using toxic cleaners, my allergies, eczema and symptoms such as coughing, sneezing, skin rashes and headaches, almost disappeared.

# Old-Fashioned Cleaners

Who would have thought that some of the everyday foods and staple ingredients we use for cooking and baking are also great natural cleaning products? And, what's more, they're cheaper and safer than the ones we buy. Lemons, vinegar and bicarbonate of soda are my absolute favourites. They're really versatile and can be used for cleaning so many things from kitchen worktops and the fridge to the bathroom sink and shower screens.

I used to love listening to my nan talking about the old days and how they would get by with limited cleaning products and everything was just fine. Sometimes the old remedies really are the best: I remember her using white vinegar, lemons and bicarbonate of soda for all sorts of things – medicinal as well as cleaning. When my eldest daughter had a particularly bad nappy rash, my nan, who was totally against using expensive baby wipes, told me to 'run a shallow, warm bath, add some bicarb and let her have a splash'. The rash would soon go, she said. And she was right. The bicarbonate of soda neutralises the acid in the bottom area caused by the baby stools and urine.

*Sometimes the old remedies really are the best.*

# Lemons

Few things can beat a lemon when it comes to getting things clean and fresh. They are naturally antibacterial, smell amazing and are kind to materials like fabric and wood. They also help get rid of water marks and traces of limescale on taps, shower screens and draining boards. Try using them to do the following:

- **Sanitise your kitchen bin.** Just mix hot water with some freshly squeezed lemon juice and rub over the bin to freshen it up.
- **Remove odours from your fridge.** Cut a lemon in half and place it, cut-side up, on a saucer inside the fridge. Change it once a week.
- **Remove grease stains from clothing.** Rub some lemon juice into the stain, let it sit overnight, and then wash as normal.
- **Clean wooden chopping boards.** Just cut a lemon in half and dip it, cut-side down, into some salt. Use to scrub the wooden boards, then rinse in warm soapy water and pat dry.
- **Polish copper pans.** Tarnished pans will be transformed if you rub them with a cut lemon dipped in salt (don't use coarse grains as they may scratch the pan). Leave for a few minutes and then rinse in warm, soapy water and dry.
- **Clean laminate worktops.** Put some lemon juice and warm water in a spray bottle. Seal and shake well before using. Wipe down with a cloth soaked in warm water, then dry.

**Caution!** Avoid using lemons on natural stone or anything that's brass-plated as the juice will damage them.

# Vinegar

Like lemons, vinegar is naturally antibacterial and great at neutralising smells. It's my go-to all-purpose cleaning aid. Try the following:

- **Prevent mould and mildew in your fridge.** Mix equal parts of white vinegar and water and use to clean inside your fridge.
- **Clean your glasses.** Use white vinegar instead of rinse aid in your dishwasher for sparkling glasses.
- **Clean chrome and stainless-steel fittings.** Just mist with undiluted white vinegar and then rub with a soft, dry cloth.
- **Remove tea and coffee stains.** Spray with distilled vinegar, then rinse and respray and rinse again before washing.

**Caution!** Always check before you spray vinegar on porous materials, such as stone or granite, and never use it to clean waxed wood. Also, *never* mix bleach and vinegar or vinegar and hydrogen peroxide. These combinations emit toxic vapours.

# Bicarbonate of soda

Also called baking soda, this leavening agent is used in baking to make cakes rise. However, it is also a fab cleaner pretty much anywhere in the home:

- **Scrub dishes and remove stains.** Sprinkle some bicarb on half a lemon and use as an abrasive cleaner.
- **Clean your hairbrushes.** Mix one teaspoon of bicarb with a little warm water and use to clean your hairbrushes.
- **Cleaner, brighter whites.** Add one small cup of bicarb to a load of laundry along with your regular detergent.

- **Minimise litter-tray odour.** Sprinkle a little bicarb in your cat-litter tray and then put the litter on top to prevent unpleasant smells.
- **Remove toilet stains.** Sprinkle some bicarb into the toilet, then spray or pour a generous amount of white vinegar around the toilet bowl and leave for 15 minutes, before scrubbing with a toilet brush.
- **Clean sinks.** For sparkling sinks, sprinkle some bicarb around the sink area and scrub with a wet sponge, then rinse well.
- **Clean plugholes.** I absolutely love the foamy goodness that white vinegar and bicarb create and they work a treat for cleaning and removing odours from plugholes. Start by pouring hot water down the plughole, then sprinkle with a couple of tablespoons of bicarb and leave for five minutes. Next pour in a glug of white vinegar and wait for 15 minutes while the magic happens, then rinse with hot water. Done regularly, this will not only mean clean plugholes, but you'll prevent blockages, too.

**Caution!** Never use a combo of bicarb and vinegar or lemon juice on your antique silver. And don't leave any leftover mixture in a sealed container – it could react and explode; be on the safe side, throw it away and wash out and dry the container for another day.

**TGCO Top Tip**

Don't forget to wear rubber gloves when using any cleaning products, homemade or commercial. They will keep your hands clean and protect them, while also maintaining soft and supple skin and preventing damage to nails.

# Cleaning with Essential Oils

Essential oils are one of the best-smelling, naturally antibacterial options for homemade cleaning products. You can add them to practically all your cleaning routines: they help sanitise the kitchen and bathroom – and no scary fumes. Aromas have such a powerful effect on our feelings and mood, too. How many times have you visited a friend's house and been welcomed with fresh scents, such as a wood-burning fire or a freshly made pot of coffee?

There are so many amazing essential oils and I love playing around with different scents. But before you purchase any, make sure that they are top quality. Essential oils are powerful, but only if they contain active compounds. So do your homework: check the labels carefully to ensure they are 100 per cent pure, with no added ingredients, and only buy from reputable companies and suppliers.

**Caution!** As with all cleaning products, test a small area before using essential oils. They can be very powerful, so extra care needs to be taken, especially if you're pregnant or have pets. Just check which oils are safe to use in different situations.

# My top essential oils for cleaning

- Cinnamon: antibacterial and antiseptic
- Eucalyptus: natural germicide
- Lavender: antibacterial
- Lemon: antiviral and antibacterial
- Peppermint: antibacterial
- Rosemary: antibacterial and antiseptic
- Tea tree: fights germs, bacteria and viruses
- Thyme: one of the most powerful oils for fighting germs
- Wild orange: great for combatting grease

# Homemade Cleaning Products

Eco-cleaning protects your health, your skin, your furniture, your pets and, of course, your environment. Why not have a go at making your own eco-cleaning products? You will save money and time shopping, plus you can also customise them with essential oils to suit your needs.

Don't forget to label them so everyone in the house knows what they are. And before you start using your DIY sprays, scrubs and solutions, give them a good shake to activate the oils. Here are some recipes for simple cleaning products I like to make.

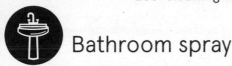

# Bathroom spray

You will need:

1 clean large spray bottle (reuse one from an old cleaning
product and stick on a new label)
200ml boiled water (that has been allowed to cool)
200ml white vinegar
5 10 drops essential oil

1. Mix the water and vinegar in the spray bottle.
2. Add the essential oil, screw on the top and give it a good
   shake.
3. Voila! You're ready to go.

Substitute this for a regular bathroom cleaner, shaking before
each use to activate the essential oil. Store in a cool, dark
cupboard.

# Carpet and fabric cleaner

Cleaning your carpets doesn't have to cost the earth if you use my
special formula. It may be cheap as chips, but it works wonders
spot-cleaning furniture and erasing stains from rugs.

You will need:

1 clean large spray bottle (reuse one from an old cleaning
product and stick on a new label)
1 tsp gentle eco washing-up liquid
1 tbsp white vinegar
250ml warm water
1 tsp bicarbonate of soda

1. Pour everything into the spray bottle, screw on the top and shake vigorously.
2. Spray the affected area and gently dab and clean. You will start to see results pretty quickly.

**Note:** Always be sure to do a small spot check before tackling big stains.

 ## Multi-purpose cleaner

This is so useful – I can't live without it. It's great for anything from cleaning floors and kitchen worktops to bathrooms.

You will need:

1 clean large spray bottle (reuse one from an old cleaning product and stick on a new label)
1–2 drops gentle eco washing-up liquid
400ml boiled water (that has been allowed to cool)
100ml white vinegar
5 drops lemon essential oil
5 drops orange essential oil

1. Add the washing-up liquid and boiled water to the spray bottle.
2. Add the vinegar and essential oils, screw the top on to the bottle and shake well.

 ## Autumn-scented cleaner

During autumn I love using this mixture for cleaning my house, especially to remove grease and grime. It has such a fresh natural scent. To make it you will need:

1 clean large spray bottle (reuse one from an old cleaning
product and stick on a new label)
100ml white vinegar
5 drops cinnamon essential oil
Peeled zest of 1 orange (in large pieces)
400ml boiled water (that has been allowed to cool)

1.  Put everything in the spray bottle, screw on the top and
    shake well.

 # Window and mirror cleaner

Windows are a workout and I prefer breathing in something
refreshing and invigorating when I'm doing mine, rather than a
commercial window cleaner. Citrus or lavender essential oil
would work well here, too. To make it you will need:

100ml white vinegar
200ml boiled water (that has been allowed to cool)
15 drops peppermint essential oil

1.  Put everything in the spray bottle, screw on the top and
    shake well.

**TGCO Top Tip**

My nan used this for cleaning her windows
along with some crumpled-up newspaper,
which works a treat. Be sure to use only black
and white newspapers, though, not coloured
ones. And don't clean windows when the sun
is shining on them and they're warm, or the
streaks will show when they dry.

# Leather and wood cleaner

All it takes to keep your leather clean and supple and your wood polished is this simple mixture. Once you've tried it, you'll never use anything else.

You will need:

1 clean large spray bottle (reuse one from an old cleaning product and stick on a new label)
120ml light olive oil
10 drops lemon essential oil

1.  Combine the olive oil and essential oil in the spray bottle, then simply spray onto a damp microfibre cloth and wipe the surface of the leather or wood.

TGCO
Top Tip

You can also use this for cleaning shoes. Apply with a thick cotton cloth, leave for a few minutes and then wipe off any residue. Buff with a clean, dry cloth.

# Kettle cleaner

Cleaning a kettle or coffee maker is easy when you know how. Here's my foolproof recipe:

480ml water
60ml white vinegar

1. Pour the water and vinegar into the kettle and bring to the boil.
2. Leave to cool, then empty and wipe with a clean cloth.
3. Rinse thoroughly with cold water and you're ready to go.

 # Oven cleaner

Cleaning your oven with some shop-bought oven cleaners can be one of the most toxic things you can do in your home. But with bicarbonate of soda, water and some good old-fashioned elbow grease, you can have a sparkling oven without resorting to unpleasant chemicals.

1. Coat the oven with bicarb, then spray with water until the powder becomes damp.
2. Leave for a couple of hours and continue spraying the bicarb as it starts to dry. This mixture will break down the grease and grime.
3. Remove the bicarb, rinse the area with warm water and hey presto – a shiny, clean oven.

 # Dishwasher cleaner

This will make your machine sparkle and smell divine.

You will need:

Hot, soapy water
White vinegar
2–3 tbsp bicarbonate of soda
4–5 drops lemon essential oil

1. Empty your dishwasher and use a sponge dipped in hot, soapy water to clean around the door edges.
2. Next, rinse and clean the filter, using the hot, soapy water.
3. Place a small glass bowl in the top rack and pour in the white vinegar.
4. Close the door and run the dishwasher on a hot cycle. This will clean the machine, removing all traces of grease, grime and musty odours.
5. When the cycle has finished, sprinkle the bicarb and lemon essential oil over the floor of the dishwasher and run a short hot-water cycle. The machine will be fresh-smelling with a bright, stain-free interior.

##  Washing-machine cleaner

Try this to keep your washing machine fresh and in great condition.

You will need:

Hot, soapy water
White vinegar
2 tbsp bicarbonate of soda
2 drops essential oil (rosemary, peppermint, lemon or any citrus oil)

1. Empty the machine and wipe around the rubber rim with hot, soapy water.
2. Remove the laundry detergent drawer and give this a good clean in your kitchen sink with hot, soapy water.
3. Before replacing the drawer in the machine, use an old toothbrush and a little white vinegar to clean the cavity it slots into. This works a treat.

4. Pour the white vinegar into the detergent drawer, sprinkle the bicarbonate of soda into the drum with a couple of drops of essential oil (I use rosemary, but you might prefer peppermint, lemon or any citrus oil) and then run the machine.

**TGCO Top Tip** Always leave the washing-machine door open to dry fully between washes.

## Tumble-dryer fragrance

If you want your clothes to have a lovely scent without having to use a fabric conditioner or artificially fragranced drying sheets, simply add a few drops of your favourite essential oil to a damp, clean cloth and place it inside the machine. I like to use lavender or geranium.

## Vacuum deodoriser

If you have a bagless vacuum cleaner, add a cotton wool ball with a few drops of essential oil, such as lavender, to the filter. The scent will waft pleasantly around the room every time you use it. For other cleaners, try inserting some orange peel inside a new vacuum bag before attaching it – trust me, it smells better than any unnatural fragrance.

**TGCO Top Tip**

Store your cleaning bottles in a safe, dark place (to protect the essential oils, which can oxidise in sunlight), such as under the kitchen sink. If you have young children or pets, fit the cupboard door with a childproof safety-lock device.

*Eco-cleaning protects your health, your skin, your furniture, your pets and, of course, your environment.*

# Troubleshooting

No matter how careful, organised, clean and tidy you are, accidents will always happen, unpleasant odours will develop and grease and grime will accumulate. However, there's no need to worry because TGCO is on hand to help you out with some eco-friendly solutions. There are very few problems that some elbow grease and troubleshooting can't solve.

# Freshen up your upholstery

If you have children or pets, you'll know that keeping upholstery clean, especially in the living room, is an ongoing challenge. Grubby feet, pet hair, dropped food and spilled drinks all take their toll, so regular cleaning is a must. This might sound like a bit of a drag and yet another chore to add to your already long to-do list, but I promise it won't take you long and the results will make it all worthwhile.

To clean my sofa and armchairs I like to use my eco-cleaning solutions, rather than buy commercial products. As far as I'm concerned, the fewer potentially toxic fumes and hazardous ingredients my family come into contact with the better. And that's why I love my special upholstery solution. It's pure, harmless, cheap and easy to make. And it's the best!

Just mix a ratio of 70 per cent boiled water (that has been allowed to cool) to 30 per cent white vinegar in a bowl and use to steam clean your upholstery. Leave to dry and job done. It will refresh the fabric's surface and kill off any bacteria and dust mites it might be harbouring.

If you don't have a steam cleaner, maybe now is the time to consider getting one. They are widely available, inexpensive and perfect for tackling even the most challenging and problematic cleaning situations. And, best of all, they eliminate the need for chemicals as the steam kills most germs, fleas and dust mites.

# Eliminate odours

Do your fabrics and cushions smell stale from constant use or lingering cigarette smoke? No worries. TGCO has some eco-friendly ways to remove those unpleasant odours. Did you know that two simple ingredients – white vinegar and bicarbonate of soda – are fab at neutralising bad odours? Just do the following and in half an hour your fabrics will smell fresh, like new.

1. Mix equal volumes of water and white vinegar in a spray bottle.
2. Screw on the top and lightly spray the fabric. Don't worry if the white vinegar smells pretty potent – it will be odourless when it dries.
3. Now shake some bicarbonate of soda over the top and leave for 30 minutes before vacuuming.

Mission accomplished! The odour will be gone ... no nasty chemicals needed.

## Stain removal

If you drop or spill something on some fabric, a rug or carpet, act fast. The longer a stain sits, the more it sets. The golden rules to follow when tackling stains are as follows:

1. Remove as much of the stain as possible.
2. Blot, scrape and scratch, but try to avoid rubbing, as this can push the stain even deeper into the fibres.
3. Always use cool water – hot water is more likely to set a stain.

Here's a guide to removing specific stains:

- **Coffee, tea, wine and other tannin stains:** try white vinegar or glycerine, but if these don't work, use a safe and biodegradable enzymatic cleaner.
- **Ink and blood:** soak the stained item overnight in a bowl of milk or a mixture of milk and white vinegar.
- **Lipstick and make-up:** glycerine can be great for dabbing on these stains, but take care not to go beyond the edges.

- **Wax, chewing gum:** freeze the area, then chip it off. An alternative for wax stains (*not* for gum) is to iron them between kitchen paper towels: the iron heats up the wax and the paper absorbs it.
- **Rings around shirt collars and perspiration:** use a shampoo that is specially formulated to remove body oils.
- **Urine, vomit and the really gross stuff:** vinegar is a great place to start, but if this doesn't work, resort to enzymatic cleaners to get rid of the nasty stuff.
- **Grass:** frothy and eco-friendly hydrogen peroxide is a greener alternative to standard chlorine bleach, and it's a wonder at removing tough grass stains.
- **Berries:** white vinegar works well on these stubborn stains.

TGCO
Top Tip

**Coffee and tea stains on cups:** you can remove the stains that build up inside cups and mugs by applying some white vinegar on a sponge.

# Keeping Your Home Pet Clean

We all love our pets – they're valued members of the family – but there's no denying that they can make our homes dirtier, hairier and smellier. If you follow TGCO's simple advice and tips, however, you can keep your home clean, free of unwanted hair and smelling fresh. And you can do all of this without resorting to harsh chemicals, which can be dangerous for pets, as well as for you, your family and the environment.

For me, making a simple switch to eco-friendly products and home remedies was a no-brainer. After all, what do dogs and cats like to do most? Groom and lick themselves. And as a cat owner, I didn't want my feline babies walking around my house and licking harmful toxic chemicals off their paws.

The way you care for your pets can have a major impact on your home environment. But don't worry – it's easy to manage and it's not rocket science. Dogs tend to get dirtier than cats and many breeds have long-haired coats that need regular grooming. So, get organised and set up a grooming station for your dog when he gets home after a walk:

- Invest in a heavy-duty doormat in your porch or entrance hall.
- Fill a plastic container or box with some old towels, a brush for getting rid of dried mud, cloths, water-spray bottles, grooming brushes and combs and a packet of treats.
- Get your dog accustomed to being cleaned and groomed after walks, so he stands still and patiently while you clean him up. Don't forget to reward him for his good behaviour with a treat.

# Bath time

If your dog is especially muddy when he arrives home, then it's straight off to the shower or bath. Not all dogs love bath time, so this can be a challenging experience for both of you. Traditional pet shampoos contain harsh chemicals and alcohol, which can cause irritations, dryness, rashes and allergic reactions, but an eco-friendly one will make it less stressful and kinder on your pet's skin. Look for shampoos with all-natural ingredients, such as aloe vera, vitamin E, coconut, honey, oatmeal and lavender.

**Note:** avoid products containing tea tree oil, which can be toxic to dogs.

## Protect your furniture and carpets

* If your pooch or puss is allowed to sit on the couch or a favourite armchair, then cover it with a nice throw to protect it from unwanted hair, dirt and odours. Then you can simply wash or clean the throw as and when necessary. Teach your pet that this is their special place to sit and sleep.
* Vacuum the carpets, rugs and furniture regularly to prevent a build-up of unwanted hair and dirt.
* Keep on top of flea treatments for your pet – mark them on the calendar and don't miss a date. You don't want infestations in your home.

## Removing pet odours

Keeping your pet's toys, beds, blankets, collars and leads clean will help to prevent strong odours inside your home; and if they are machine washable, so much the better. Save this chore for a sunny or breezy day when they can be dried outside in the fresh air. For furniture and upholstery that isn't easy to clean, a light spray of vodka will help remove any unwanted odours. Bicarbonate of soda is also great at neutralising smells; you can shake it over rugs and carpets before vacuuming or leave pots of it in offending areas to absorb local smells. Vinegar is another eco-friendly solution – I like to use it when washing pets' toys and bedding.

# Keeping Your Home Baby- and Child-Friendly

As soon as your baby is ready to start crawling, you'll become more aware of how dirty your floors and carpets are and the germs, bacteria and other health hazards they may harbour. I remember worrying about this when I had my first daughter, but, luckily, my nan was on hand to bring me down to earth and reassure me that 'a little bit of dirt won't hurt her'. This was her generation's attitude to cleaning and it mostly served them well. Nevertheless, I wanted to keep my home clean and protect my baby from absolutely everything, especially dirt and grime.

I took it a bit too far! The first thing I did was to introduce a no-shoe policy for everyone entering my home – I didn't want dirt from outdoor footwear adding to the problem. I vacuumed the carpets twice a day – first thing every morning and last thing at night – and mopped the floor in the evening. I even considered attaching little dusters to my daughter's knees at one point to assist me with my cleaning duties but, surprise, surprise, this seemed a step too far and I quickly abandoned the idea. There is nothing to be gained from overdoing it!

Babies and young children have sensitive skin, so in order to prevent any unnecessary irritation, always be careful when choosing detergents. Obviously, disinfecting the floors and keeping them clean is very important when your baby is crawling, but there are lots of safe child-friendly options available to minimise any risks, including specially formulated eco-products that don't contain harsh and potentially toxic chemicals.

Alternatively, it takes no time at all to make your own cleaning products with safe everyday ingredients from your kitchen cupboards. Here's my simple solution for cleaning, killing germs and making floors safe for babies and toddlers.

# My homemade child-friendly floor cleaner

1.  Combine 120ml white vinegar with 4.8 litres warm water in a clean bucket.
2.  Mix well before using to mop the floor.

The acetic acid content of the vinegar will kill the bacteria and act as a disinfectant. You could also add five drops of essential oil to the solution if you want to make it more fragrant and have lovely fresh-smelling floors.

**TGCO Top Tip**

Steam mops are fab for disinfecting surfaces and removing a wide range of stains. You can use them with my homemade child-friendly floor cleaner (above).

# 10 ways to . . .
## clean and shop green

Here are some practical tips on how to become an eco-warrior and make your contribution to saving the planet.

## 1.
### KNOW WHAT YOU'RE BUYING

You need to be careful about which cleaning products you use. You don't want to be breathing in toxins – or flushing them into our oceans.

## 2.
### MAKE YOUR OWN CLEANING PRODUCTS

Try, whenever you can, to make your own cleaning products. They're so easy to put together and you'll know exactly what is in them (see the recipes on pp. 126–34).

## 3.
### GET CREATIVE WITH ESSENTIAL OILS

So often, we love buying cleaning products because of their smells. But it's just as easy to buy some good-quality essential oils and add these to white vinegar to clean your house (see the recipes on pp. 126–34). Or maybe add some lemon juice or orange zest for a citrusy touch. Get creative and experiment to see which smells you and your family like the most.

# 4.

## GO OLD-SCHOOL AND USE YOUR GROCERIES TO CLEAN

Lemons, vinegar and bicarbonate of soda are great for cleaning (see pp. 122–4). They're so versatile and you've probably already got them all at home.

# 5.

## BUY LOOSE FRUIT AND VEGETABLES IN PAPER BAGS AND AVOID EXCESSIVE FOOD PACKAGING

We all know the damage that plastic is causing to our environment. Buying loose fruit and veg is one of the easiest ways to fight this.

# 6.

## TAKE A BAG WITH YOU EVERY TIME YOU GO SHOPPING

Keep one in your handbag. Keep one in your coat pocket. Keep one in the boot of your car. If you have bags on hand, you won't ever need to pay for them, and you'll be helping our planet.

# 7.

## TAKE YOUR OWN REUSABLE COFFEE CUP TO THE BARISTA IN YOUR LOCAL COFFEE SHOP

So many coffee shops now offer you a discount if you bring your own cup. Though it might seem slightly strange at first, you'll be saving a little on every coffee, which can add up over a month, plus you'll be helping the environment too.

# 8.

## CHOOSE ALUMINIUM CANS INSTEAD OF PLASTIC BOTTLES

Even though companies are starting to make great products out of recycled plastic bottles, we all still need to limit our consumption. Get yourself a reusable water bottle and if you do find yourself craving a soft drink, buy it in a can.

# 9.

## SWITCH TO REUSABLE SANDWICH BAGS

Another easy way to use less plastic is to buy dishwasher-safe reusable sandwich bags. I also like using beeswax food wraps instead of cling film and plastic wrap. All little things that can make a big difference.

# 10.

## SAY NO TO PLASTIC STRAWS AND CUTLERY

Carry a small spoon and fork in your handbag or keep them in your desk at work. If you really can't give up using straws, use paper or reusable ones.

# 4: Upcycling and Donating

Whenever I declutter, I'm always mindful about not throwing things away into the bin, especially now that we're all increasingly aware of the dangers of climate change, global warming, polluted seas and overflowing landfill sites. Embracing a more sustainable, kinder and ethical lifestyle is so important. I believe that we all have a duty to look after our planet, and I try to educate and inform my clients while we declutter together, offering advice and tips on how they can do this in their everyday lives.

No matter how small they may seem, all our individual contributions do add up and have a positive impact. They show that we care and we're all stakeholders in the future of our planet and mankind. So, if you think you can't make a difference, think again.

# Upcycling

This is a very good place to start. Every time you upcycle an item you give it a new lease of life. With a sprinkle of creativity, you can take something you no longer need or use and give it a new purpose, making it unique.

Here's an example of what I mean. TGCO always recommends using dividers in bedroom drawers to keep everything neat and tidy. That way, when you put your clean undies away, it will be an enjoyable experience, rather than a chore sorting everything out yet again. However, you don't have to make a special trip to the shops to buy expensive, specially made drawer dividers. You can upcycle instead, reusing cardboard food boxes: just cut them down to fit inside your drawers and hey presto. You're organised. And if you're creative and stylish, you could even cover them in a pretty fabric.

I hate waste and love repurposing all sorts of things, often in highly inventive ways. Here are lots of ideas to help and inspire you. Nothing will get wasted in your home now you're learning to upcycle.

## Plastic food containers

Are you as sick of throwing away plastic food containers as I am? It's almost impossible to buy things in the supermarket that aren't packaged in plastic. But TGCO has a mega tip for reusing plastic boxes that will help keep your fridge clean and organised like never before. To upcycle the boxes from grapes, berries or mushrooms, simply wash them out in warm, soapy water, dry with a tea towel and place in your fridge drawers ready for storing your veg and fruit. This is much neater than shoving things in wrapped in brown paper or plastic bags, and you can easily see the contents.

# Old glass candle jars

These can be recycled and turned into containers for cotton buds (make sure these are the biodegradable ones), make-up removal pads or make-up brushes. Simply pour hot water into the glass jar and leave for an hour; once the water has cooled down, the wax should have risen to the top of the jar. Then pop it out and leave to one side (it can be placed in a small bag to scent your linen drawers), give the glass jar a clean with some warm, soapy water and you have a new glass container.

# Plastic-bag samosas

'What?' I hear you ask. 'Has TGCO taken leave of her senses?' Actually, it's the opposite, as this is a brilliant idea for upcycling all those plastic bags that are lying around your house.

Every day, I do my best to say no to plastic bags, but despite my best efforts, they still manage to creep into my home. So instead of letting them take over or chucking them out, I simply transform them into plastic-bag 'samosas' – the perfect carrier-bag triangle pouches! They look fab, they save space (especially if you store them inside your kitchen drawers or cupboards), they're easy to grab when you need them and, best of all, you can keep them inside your handbag or even a pocket for when you pop out to the shops. Try it and see for yourself (you can thank me later).

To fold your very own carrier-bag 'samosa', just follow my step-by-step instructions:

1. Take a plastic carrier bag and smooth it out flat.
2. Working from the edge of one long side, fold a long section (one-third of the width of the bag) over towards the middle, then fold again and repeat one

last time until you end up with a long thin rectangle, three folds thick.

3. Now comes the clever bit. Working from one short end of the rectangle, fold over the right-hand corner to align with the left-hand edge into a triangle. Keep folding in triangles along the length of the section until you end up with a thick triangle and a small piece of plastic left over.

4. Tuck the leftover plastic securely inside the folds to make a neat 'samosa'.

5. Repeat with all your plastic bags and store the samosas away in an easily accessible place. You'll always have a bag on hand when you need one.

*Say no to new plastic carrier bags and always carry your own plastic-bag 'samosas'. Don't get caught short!*

## Tin cans

Tin cans are so versatile and can be reused in so many ways, so don't throw your empty ones in the recycling bin. Instead, wash them thoroughly in warm, soapy water, then rinse and dry. Leave them *au naturel*, if you like their shiny steel finish, or spray paint them in the colour of your choice. Then use for planting herbs or flowers to put on the windowsill and brighten up your kitchen or for storing utensils. Alternatively, you can transform them into attractive holders for patio lights. Just use a hammer and nail to make a pretty pattern of holes through which the light can shine.

Who would have thought that a humble tin could be so useful?

# Cardboard boxes

If these are in good condition, they make fabulous storage baskets for storing towels, linen, kids' toys, paperwork, etc. Just follow these instructions:

1. Cut off the flaps around the top of the box and throw them in the recycling bin.
2. Starting from the base, take a roll of thick brown string and wrap it around the side of the box, working your way up to the top edge, until the box is covered. Use a hot glue gun to secure the ends of the string to the box to stop it unravelling.
3. If you're a dab hand at sewing, you could upcycle an old pillowcase as a lining.

# Clothes hangers

Next time you declutter your wardrobe and are left with a bunch of unused clothes or trouser hangers, put a couple aside for a quick crafts project. Just add two clothes pegs to each hanger and use as a recipe holder. Easy peasy.

## Designer gift boxes

You may have a collection of upmarket gift boxes in different shapes and sizes that once held stuff such as posh candles, cosmetics and scent. We often hang on to them 'just in case' because 'they might come in handy one day'. Well, now's the time to reuse them as the perfect organising trays for underwear and toiletries inside your chest of drawers.

*Nothing will get wasted in your home now you're learning to upcycle.*

## Water bottles

If you enjoy watching the birds that visit your garden, you can reuse empty plastic water bottles (with caps) as bird feeders. Here's what you do:

1. Wash out the bottle and remove the label. Pat dry.
2. Punch two holes on opposite sides of the bottle near the bottom and insert a wooden stick or chopstick into one hole, passing it through the bottle and out of the hole on the other side. This will become a perch for feeding birds.
3. Repeat the process to make another perch just above the first one.
4. Punch a small hole in the bottle about 4cm above each perch. These are the feeding holes, so they shouldn't be too

big – just large enough to allow the birds to access the seeds inside the feeder.

5. Make two holes on opposite sides of the neck of the bottle and thread some sturdy string through them to make a hanger. Tie the ends in a knot.

6. Fill the bottle with mixed seeds, then screw on the cap and hang the feeder from the branch of a tree (well out of reach of any local cats).

## Washing-capsule containers

Old washing-capsule containers are a great under-the-sink storage solution. Fill them with cleaning cloths, sponges, scrubbers and dishwasher tablets.

# Donating

Nothing makes clearing clutter easier or more worthwhile than knowing your unwanted or surplus household items, clothes and shoes are going to a worthy cause. That's why donating is such a wonderful pursuit: it frees you of all the stuff you no longer need, while helping other people.

Here TGCO highlights some of the most popular things you can give away, with suggestions for suitable recipients and tips on what to do before you donate.

# Books

If you find it difficult to give away your beloved books, I've got a few solutions to help you:

- Identify the books you really love and reread – the ones that have made a difference to your life – and give them a prominent place on your bookshelves. Display them and enjoy them.
- Sort through your non-fiction books – dictionaries, atlases, reference books, cookbooks, gardening books and practical instruction manuals – and keep those that you love or use and refer to regularly.
- Go through all the children's books your kids have grown out of. If they're not going to read them again and you're not planning on having more babies, put them in the 'donate' pile.

The books that are left over – those that you're not reading and are unlikely to use again – are 'good to go' and can be donated. Knowing they'll go to a 'good home' makes the decluttering task much easier. Now here are some ideas for where to take them:

- Local schools, hospitals and doctors' surgeries and waiting areas.
- Local libraries – most will be glad to take your books.
- Most high-street charity shops.
- Specialist organisations and charities, such as Books2Africa.

# Clothes and shoes

As with books and other personal and precious possessions, knowing that your clothes are going to a worthy cause makes parting with them much easier. Keep a donation bag or box inside your wardrobe for all the things you haven't worn in a while. Make sure they're clean and aren't missing buttons or need mending before adding them to the pile. Anything you donate should be in good condition. When the bag's full, you can donate the contents to one of the following:

- Local charity and hospice shops
- Recycling/reuse centres
- Homeless charities and women's refuges
- Children's charities
- Specialist charities for elderly people and for unemployed people who need work clothes for attending job interviews
- Some clothing chains take in bags of clean clothes and you will be given a voucher to spend in-store in exchange

# Underwear

New and used clean bras and knickers can be donated to the specialist charities:

- Love Support Unite
- Smalls for All

Both of these organisations help vulnerable children and women in Africa and were set up to say 'pants to poverty'. They collect and distribute new knickers, as well as unworn or gently worn bras. Sadly, there are still many women around the world who don't even have one pair of pants or a bra, let alone a drawer full of them, and this is a major health and hygiene problem in some poor African communities. Even those girls who are fortunate enough to get an education often have to miss school days due to not having any underwear.

Underwear may also be perceived as a sign of the wearer's status and confers a degree of personal security. When a woman wears underwear, people assume that she has a male figure in her life who cares about her. Consequently, she is less vulnerable and at a lower risk of being attacked.

So, that's where my barely worn bras go. I also throw in a pack of new knickers as no woman or child should be going pant-less – it simply isn't right in this day and age.

*Donating is such a wonderful pursuit: it frees you of all the stuff you no longer need, while helping other people.*

## Make-up

Do you have lots of unused make-up and cosmetics still in its original packaging, lying around your bedroom and bathroom? Well, fear not, there are charities and non-profit initiatives that will pass it on to women at refuges. You can donate to the following:

- Some local charity shops
- Give and Makeup, which donates unwanted cosmetics and toiletries to women's shelters

- The Beauty Bank – a group that provides women, men and young people in need with the 'little luxuries' in life
- The Hygiene Bank – for hygiene essentials, beauty and personal-care products

# Computers

If you're thinking of replacing your computer with a new model, before you donate your old one, don't forget to wipe the hard drive clean and remove any personal information. (If the computer is really old and does not support modern operating systems, it's unlikely that anyone will want it and you may have to find an alternative way of disposing of it in an environmentally responsible manner.) To donate your computer to a good cause and help other people, contact the following:

- Local schools and colleges
- Your local library
- A specialist charity – Google 'donating computers to charity' to find the websites of organisations that specialise in this field
- Age UK – they will accept any working PC, desktop body, tablet, mobile phone, screen or laptop; visit their website to discover how to send your items for free

**Note:** for an easy way to recycle your electronics, you can take your old laptop, tablet or phone to an Apple or Microsoft store and, if they still have value, they'll give you credit or a gift card in exchange.

# Mobile phones

Do you have hidden treasure in the form of an old mobile phone? If so, you can recycle it and maybe earn a little bit of cash in the process. Please note that your mobile phone needs to be in reasonable condition, with no more than mild cosmetic damage, and in working order. Before recycling it, make sure that you wipe it clean to remove all your personal data. Compare & Recycle will compare quotes from top UK recycling companies.

# Furniture

Don't chop up your old furniture or take it to your local tip – donate it. In most cases, no matter how old, unfashionable or in need of a lick of paint, it can come in very useful to someone in need and help charities raise valuable funds, so think before you chuck it out. Before you donate, you should do the following: dust it, clean it, polish it and make sure that it's safe. You can donate to many organisations:

- British Heart Foundation will collect items from your home for free. You can phone to book your home collection.
- Emmaus UK doesn't just make a difference to people's lives – it also helps save the environment by recycling and reusing as much as possible and creates volunteering jobs for local people, too.
- Shelter offers support and advice to homeless people. They cannot collect furniture and have limited space in their shops, so please check first.
- YMCA helps young people with accommodation, family-support services and education and training.

- Local homeless shelters are often happy to receive old furniture. Call in advance though, to make sure they are accepting donations.

# Food

Unfortunately, food banks still exist, even in civilised and affluent societies like our own. They provide emergency food for people and families living in poverty, often due to housing loss, family breakdown and mental-health problems. Food banks rely on the general public's goodwill and support. They need our help. Here are some general suggestions for donating food; for more information and links, see Sourcebook, p. 192.

- Donate directly to your local food bank.
- You can also donate food at collection points in supermarkets across the country.
- Host a collection at a nearby local school, church or business for your local food bank or people in hunger and need.

**Note:** check the expiry dates on food before donating. Most food banks cannot give out any food that is past by its sell-by date.

# Toys

So, you want to give your kids' old toys a new life, while helping other children and decluttering your home. But where do you donate used toys to help kids in need? There are some worthy organisations just waiting for toys in good condition. Please call and check with the following before you arrive with your donations:

- The Salvation Army
- Children's hospitals and wards
- Doctors' and dentists' waiting rooms
- Women's shelters
- Children's homes
- Local social services and health visitors

## Soft toys

When you declutter the kids' bedrooms and end up with a bag full of soft toys, what do you do? TGCO has some useful tips to help you find a good home for them:

- Animal shelters – they are always grateful for soft toys, as many rescue dogs and cats love cuddling up to a teddy.
- Local women's refuges – children escaping domestic violence often turn up with nothing but the clothes they're wearing.
- The Freecycle Network, which is all about reuse and keeping good stuff out of landfills.
- Local schools for tombola prizes.

**Note:** make sure any soft toys you donate are clean or freshly washed, safe to use and in good condition.

# Tools

We often buy tools or a tool set for a specific project, but after the job's completed, they just sit in the garage or shed and collect dust, taking up valuable storage space. Luckily, there are specialist charities and organisations you can donate your tools to and they will distribute them to people who need them and for use overseas in local community projects:

- WORKAID and Tools for Self Reliance (they refurbish tools and send them to Africa)
- UK charities such as Age UK

## Linen and towels

Nearly all of us have a motley assortment of old and unused linen and towels cluttering up our airing cupboards and linen presses. Time to declutter and donate them to the following:

- Homeless shelters for items in good condition
- Local animal shelters – they can use them for bedding and bathing animals
- Local charity shops
- Social services and health visitors
- YMCA

**Note:** all linen should be washed before you donate.

TGCO
Top Tip

Be sure to call ahead to see if your local shelter is accepting donations.

## Spectacles

Eyewear is a great recycling option because glasses are always in demand:

- Vision Aid Overseas will recycle your old glasses and use the funds raised to offer optical care overseas. Just take them into your local branch of Specsavers.
- Your Lions Club may have a collection bin or you can send your old glasses to them for free or take them to a Marie Curie charity shop.

# Sourcing Local Charities

Of course, there are many causes that you can support. The Charity Retail Association can help you find charity shops in your area. Charitychoice.co.uk lists every charity in the UK by any number of searchable categories, whether by type, religion or location, for example.

**Note**: for contact details and websites of the charities, organisations and companies mentioned in this chapter, see Sourcebook, p. 191.

# *10 ways to . . .*
# upcycle

We are all guilty of throwing away perfectly good things that can be upcycled and repurposed. Let's turn over a new leaf and make a special effort to think about how an item can be reused before we chuck it in the bin. Here are some ideas to inspire you:

## 1.

### TRADE IN YOUR ITEMS

This can be a good way to make cash from unused things, while ensuring they are properly recycled. Do your research, as lots of companies will allow you to exchange containers or old items for something else.

## 2.

### DONATE RATHER THAN BIN

Always try to donate things where possible. One man's trash is another man's treasure; someone might benefit from things you don't use any more.

# 3.

## UPCYCLE

There are so many great ways to upcycle your common household items and give them a new lease of life. And you don't have to be the crafty type to do this.

# 4.

## DON'T THROW AWAY OLD SHIRTS

Use these as cleaning cloths. Or, if you're crafty, turn pretty, patterned ones into cushion covers or make a patchwork quilt.

# 5.

## DON'T THROW AWAY YOUR OLD WELLIES

You can use them as planters in your garden. Use different colours and sizes and turn them into a feature.

# 6.

## REUSE CARDBOARD TOILET ROLLS

These are great for storing wires and cables. Stand the toilet rolls upright in a shoebox, then use each one to house a cable, keeping them neat and separate.

# 7.

## REUSE CANDLE JARS

Once you've got rid of any remaining wax, these make great storage containers for your bathroom necessities or make-up brushes. You can even use them as mini vases on your bedside table.

# 8.

## REUSE MASON JARS

These are great for packed lunches. Make layered salads or keep fruit in them. You could also use them for breakfast parfaits.

# 9.

## DON'T THROW AWAY EGG CARTONS

Use these to grow your own herb garden.

# 10.

## KEEP OLD LIGHTBULBS

These can be turned into Christmas ornaments; painting and decorating them can also be a fun family activity.

# 5: Decluttering to Go: Planning a Clutter-free Holiday

There are few things I love more than planning a holiday and I've been known to start getting organised two months before even hitting the terminal. However, as extreme as that may be, there's nothing worse than a last-minute panic with insufficient time to pack, so that you end up throwing a month's worth of clothes and shoes into your suitcase for a two-night city break!

I'm here to help you out and get you packed without the drama. By being proactive, doing some simple prep and making lists of everything you need, you can help to make your dream holiday stress-free.

# Make a list

Always have a plan. And this starts with a list of everything you'll need for your trip. So, grab a pen and some paper (or use a computer, so you can go back and edit, as needed) and organise the items on your list under the following headings:

**Clothing and footwear:** tops, bottoms, dresses, swimwear, underwear, socks, pyjamas

**Accessories:** bags, belts, scarves, sunglasses, jewellery

**Toiletries:** toothbrush/paste, make-up, sunscreen, after-sun, beauty and bath products, hairbrush

**Entertainment:** tablet, headphones, chargers, portable speakers, packs of cards, books, journals

**Sports:** gym clothes, snorkel, goggles and flippers, tennis racket, golf clubs, skis

**Essentials:** passport, tickets, wallet, medication, basic first-aid kit, spectacles, adapters

Having made a list once, you can then adapt it for other trips; you don't have to start from scratch each time. If I'm going away for at least two weeks, I'll work out what I'm planning to do in more detail and organise accordingly – for instance, which outfits I'll wear once I have a tan and what to take if I'm planning any special day trips or excursions.

*By being proactive and doing some simple prep you can make your dream holiday stress-free.*

## My Golden Rule

Only make lists that make sense to *YOU*.

## Get Organised

Once I've made my lists, I get organised. I always start by getting out all my essential travel equipment, including the following:

- **A mini clothes rail** This is a fabulous item I learned about from my mother, and it makes the whole packing process much calmer. You can use it to hang up all the items you think you may want to take with you and easily plan your outfits. This will help you to decide which things are necessary and which you can do without. What's more, it takes up very little room in your home and is easy to store when not in use – no clutter allowed at TGCO HQ!
- **A lightweight or sturdy suitcase** The suitcase I use depends on where I'm going and the length of the trip. For a city break or just two to three nights away, I'll opt for a carry-on

lightweight suitcase that conforms to airlines' specifications regarding size and weight. If I'm going away for longer or flying long haul, I'll use a sturdier, larger suitcase that I can check into the hold. If I'm just going away overnight or taking the car, I'll pack a large, soft travel bag.

- **Packing cubes** I always suggest my clients buy a set of packing cubes to help keep both their suitcases and their accommodation at the other end in order. These wonderful organisers are so clever and will transform the way you pack. They come in different sizes, keep clothes neat, minimise creases and they're simple to use. You can categorise items in your suitcase and you'll find you have a lot more space. The big plus is that when you arrive at your destination you don't even need to unpack if you don't want to. Just place the cubes inside the drawers or cupboards and your room will stay tidy and organised.

*Always have a plan.*

**TGCO Top Tip**

When buying a sturdy suitcase, make sure it's tough as well as light. It will have to withstand a lot of knocks. I always recommend choosing a brightly coloured one, so it will be easier to spot on the luggage carousel and it's less likely that someone might walk off with it by mistake, which often happens to travellers with black cases. Alternatively, you can buy a vividly coloured lockable strap that fits around your case, or tie on some coloured thread.

# How to Pack

Do you enjoy packing for a holiday? If so, you're the exception rather than the rule. So many of us get stressed out when we're faced with an empty suitcase. For some people, it's nothing short of a challenge and can even trigger an anxiety attack. But there's no need to feel that way. Packing can be pleasurable if you're in control, have a tried-and-tested system that works and a detailed list of what to take (see p. 170). It's just a matter of being organised, and that's where TGCO can help. I've been there and I've got packing down to a fine art.

Here's my step-by-step guide to stress-free packing:

1.  Don't leave it to the last minute when there's not enough time and you're in a rush. Get out your suitcase and start sorting out what you need a couple of days or more in advance.

2.  Get out your mini clothes rail. Remove the clothes on your list from the wardrobe and hang them on the rail where you can see them clearly. It makes it much easier to coordinate your outfits, shoes, accessories and even your jewellery. That way, you can pack with confidence, knowing exactly what you're taking away with you while keeping your luggage-weight allowance (and your blood pressure) within the recommended limits.

3.  Get out all the other clothing items on your packing list. Arrange them in categories – sweaters, T-shirts, jeans, swimwear, underwear, socks and tights, etc. – on your bed or a flat surface, ready to pack.

4.  Start off by rolling up or neatly folding your clothes. Rolling is one of the best suitcase-packing tips, and for good reason. It compresses your clothes, so you can fit more in and also makes them easier to find. I recommend rolling softer clothes, such as underwear, T-shirts and beachwear.

These won't wrinkle when they're rolled up tightly. Fold everything that's made from stiffer fabrics, e.g. shirts, trousers and blazers, or things that crease easily.

5. Pack the rolled-up clothes neatly into the packing cubes and zip them up, then place in the bottom of the suitcase.

6. Next place your shoes around the cubes, making sure they're paired together. You might find it helpful to put them in soft shoe bags.

7. Pack your toiletry and make-up bags in the zipped portion of the suitcase, so they can be held more firmly in place. To be on the safe side in case of leakages, place bottles of shampoo, moisturiser, lotions, gels, cleansers, etc., in plastic bags inside the toiletry bag.

8. Lastly, place the folded clothes on top, starting with the longest pieces like dresses, shirts and trousers, and stack them on top of each other. I always place the items I'll need first right at the top, like my kaftan, bikini and hat – it's so simple!

TGCO
Top Tip

Slip a clean sock over coarsely bristled brushes, so they won't tear into clothes or mark your favourite shoes.

**TGCO Top Tip**

To avoid the stress of packing when you're coming home from your holiday, pack as you go along. Once clothes are dirty, roll them and put them back in your suitcase. You might have to do a big load of laundry when you get home, but you'll have much less stuff in your hotel room to deal with.

**TGCO Top Tip**

**Vacuum-pack your clothes:** vacuum bags are one of the best investments you'll ever make. They will save space at home storing duvets and bulky clothes, as well as protecting them from moths and bugs. And when it comes to squeezing a lot of stuff into your suitcase they come into their own. You just put your clothes inside, seal them and squeeze the air out, so they pack really flat. What's not to like?

## Your toiletry bag

We all love to take as many toiletries on holiday as possible, but with all the airline weight restrictions, it's best to decide exactly which items you will need and then to pack them in an organised but streamlined way. I suggest you take just one make-up bag and one toiletry bag. As long as you're stocked up on the essential items, don't stress too much about forgetting things. You can always buy anything else you need at the airport or when you arrive at your destination. Many large hotels even have a shop that sells basic toiletries.

I'm a great fan of miniature travel bottles as they take up much less space in a suitcase and weigh less than standard ones. You can either buy special travel-sized beauty products (but they can be quite pricey and aren't great for the environment) or you can upcycle small plastic bottles (or buy specially designed small bottles with screw tops or sprays) and fill them with the items already in your bathroom cupboard. The beauty of these bottles is that they can be reused again and again.

# Your hand luggage

I always try to keep hand luggage as light as possible. I don't want to lug a heavy bag around the airport with me, nor do I want to unpack all my holiday stuff when I'm going through security. All you need is your passport, boarding pass, purse/wallet, sunglasses, phone, any medication you may have to take and a good book, plus optional items such as travel-insurance documents, headphones and sweets to suck if your ears pop.

If you're on a hand-baggage-only holiday, then TGCO recommends you place your toiletry bag at the top of your case or in an outer compartment, so you can easily access it at security. Stocking up on clear plastic bags for your liquids before arriving at the airport will save you having to do it under pressure. Make sure all bottle tops are screwed on tightly – spillages could ruin your trip.

**TGCO Top Tip**

A beach bag can be quite large and it can be tricky getting one into your suitcase once all your clothes, shoes and toiletries are neatly stowed away, so I have a great solution: I use mine for hand luggage. If you're packing for a holiday in the sun, and having problems fitting everything in, this tip can be a game-changer.

**TGCO Top Tip**

Place your passport and important travel documents in a small clutch bag or soft cloth bag inside your carry-on bag. This not only gives them a home but also keeps them separate from your money and enables you to access them easily and quickly when checking in and passing through security and immigration control.

*TGCO will make all your family-travel anxieties disappear.*

# Travelling with Kids and Babies

Just thinking about what needs to be taken when travelling with children is enough to make even the most organised parent break into a cold sweat. And when you're en-route to the airport, surrounded by suitcases, hand luggage, buggies, car seats and other equipment, you might seriously consider turning around and heading back home. But fear not, TGCO is here to make all your family-travel anxieties disappear.

## Pack a grown-ups' bag

First things first: start by packing yourself a grown-ups' bag in which you'll keep all the essential items that the adults need. This way, both you and your partner will know exactly where all the important travel-related items are located. This bag should contain the following:

- Passports
- Travel documents
- Insurance documents
- Hotel/accommodation confirmation
- Tickets
- Purse/wallet
- Sunglasses
- Phone, tablet, iPod, Kindle and chargers

# Pack a children's essentials bag

This bag will contain all the necessities for the duration of the trip from your home to where you will be staying. The contents will vary depending on how old your children are. Don't pack separate bags for each child. This is just more work for you, more bags to carry, plus possible duplication and confusion. You don't want the burden of taking the kids to the bathroom, one a time, with several different bags, so just pack one essentials bag to take care of as many people as possible. This bag should include any or all of the following, depending on your children's ages:

- Disposable nappies and nappy bags
- Baby wipes and cream
- Bottles and baby milk
- Jars of baby food and plastic spoons
- Dummy and comfort blanket
- Infant suspension pain relief in small bottle (less than 100ml)
- Extra underwear and one set of spare clothes per child
- Toothbrush and toothpaste

**Note:** when travelling by plane with a baby, you're allowed to take in your hand luggage enough sterilised water, baby milk, powdered formula and baby food as you need for the journey. Each container will be screened when you pass through security.

Most airlines allow you to take a buggy and travel cot or car seat for free. You'll be able to push your child through the airport in the buggy, but you will probably have to fold it away and check it in at the gate. Invest in a buggy bag to protect it on the flight. And remember that a buggy is great for transporting equipment and lunch/snack boxes – you can store them underneath or behind or hang them from the handles.

## Pack a children's rucksack

I recommend packing a rucksack with things to keep toddlers and older children happy and occupied on the journey, so that it is as stress-free as possible. This bag should include the following:

- Your child's favourite snacks
- Divided lunch box full of finger-friendly foods
- Drinks (under 100ml)
- Bottle and baby milk cartons
- Small toys and a colouring pack
- Soft, lightweight blanket to stay warm and snuggly
- Children's tablet with lots of games and movies downloaded on to it

**TGCO Top Tip** Taking some new toys for toddlers (as well as old favourites) will help keep them entertained.

# A note about snacks

Most airports sell all types of snacks for babies and children. I always kept a selection handy in my bag to whip out if one of my kids was on the verge of having a complete meltdown. Don't get me wrong; I know snacking shouldn't be used as a comforter, but when you're travelling and your child is about to disrupt the peace and quiet of your fellow passengers, who are trying to sleep or relax, you can give her as many Percy Pigs as she wants!

*There are so many ways to pack for a holiday, but if you're organised and think ahead, you'll feel really chilled and relaxed when you step onto the plane.*

# And Finally ...

When you return home, happy and relaxed after a great holiday, do as I do and put all the things you only use when you're travelling in a packing cube in your empty suitcase, together with your packing lists, ready for next time. That way, you won't forget any of your essential items or waste valuable time looking for them. There are so many ways to pack for a holiday, but if you're organised and think ahead, it'll make your life so much easier and you'll feel really chilled and relaxed when you step onto the plane. Happy travels!

# 10 ways to . . .
## prep and pack

Travelling will be a breeze, even with young children, if you do it the TGCO way:

## 1.

### MAKE A PACKING LIST

A comprehensive packing list will give you peace of mind and make sure you cover all the essentials. If it works better for you, you can make a master list and just edit it slightly for different trips (e.g. weekend city break vs summer beach holiday).

## 2.

### ROLL OR VACUUM-PACK YOUR CLOTHES

This will help prevent creases and give you more space in your suitcase. Be sure to fold items that may crease easily though.

## 3.

### USE PACKING CUBES

These will help you keep your clothes organised while travelling and at your destination. Simply pop the cubes straight in the drawers at the other end and your accommodation will stay tidy and manageable.

# 4.

## KEEP YOUR CLOTHES SMELLING FRESH

My favourite way to do this is to put a few drops of an essential oil onto a handkerchief and tuck it into the suitcase.

# 5.

## WEIGH YOUR LUGGAGE

You don't want to get to the airport and find that you've packed too much and have to spend a fortune on excess-baggage fees. Make sure you weigh your luggage before you leave the house to check it is within the limit.

# 6.

## BUY A LIGHTWEIGHT COLOURFUL SUITCASE

Keep the kilos down with a lightweight suitcase. The less it weighs, the more clothes you can bring with you. We all know that I love a rainbow, but a colourful suitcase will be easier to pick out from the sea of greys and blacks on the baggage carousel.

# 7.

## GO DIGITAL

Books can be bulky and heavy, but bytes weigh nothing at all. Download reading material, maps, translation apps, travel guides and games on to your phone or tablet.

# 8.

## DON'T OVERPACK

We all want to protect against worst-case travel scenarios, but try to avoid bringing too much. While it's smart to carry, say, a small first-aid kit, you can't pack for every possible crisis.

# 9.

## KEEP CABLES AND WIRES TIDY

Secure them individually with cable ties and pack in an easy-to-spot pouch. Put your laptop and smartphone charger in your hand baggage for safekeeping.

# 10.

## WHEN FLYING WITH KIDS, PACK SNACKS AND TOYS

Use a divided box with plenty of finger foods. Distracting your children with fun snack time is a great way to make flying easier.

# One Last Thing

I hope you've enjoyed reading *Mind Over Clutter* as much as I've enjoyed writing it, sharing my work, top tips and experiences with you. At first, I wasn't sure how I'd fit this in while wearing my mum/wife/organiser/blogger hats. There are only so many hours in the day, so how could I add an author hat to all the others? But there was no need to worry. In the end, it all came down to good planning, making some short-term sacrifices – and lots of music! Music helps my soul grow and puts me in such a happy place ...

Decluttering and organising are a way of life for me, but I do understand that they're not for everyone and some of you may find them challenging. However, I've written this book in such a way that you can drop in and out whenever you want and find exactly what you need to know. You don't have to read it from cover to cover, although it would be great if you do, of course!

What really blows my mind is that this book is mine. I never dreamed that this would ever happen, especially as I only started my business a short time ago, back when no one was talking about decluttering. But now I receive so many amazing messages from my clients and followers on social media, asking for help and sharing photos of their cupboards, drawers, wardrobes and homes. I can't tell you how happy this makes me, nor can I thank you all enough for embracing TGCO and supporting what I do. I know for a fact that dreams really do come true if you work incredibly hard, wear all those hats and believe in yourself. You can do it – and you can achieve anything!

*Nicola Lewis x*

- #thisgirlcanorganise
- #tgco
- #mindoverclutter
- #mumslife
- #declutterchallenge
- #youcandoit
- #removetheclutter
- #everythinginitsplace
- #organisedhome
- #keepwhatyoulove
- #positiveattitude

Nicola comes in and, without judging you, she gets your house in order. 'Organised room, organised mind' really is true – because as soon as Nicola has worked her magic, it's like a weight has been lifted and you can think clearly and stop closing doors to avoid certain rooms. You actually fall in love with your home all over again.

— ANONYMOUS CLIENT

# References

1.  https://www.nytimes.com/2019/01/03/well/mind/clutter-stress-procrastination-psychology.html
2.  https://undecidedthebook.files.wordpress.com/2012/07/saxbe-repetti-pspb-2010.pdf
3.  https://www.sleepfoundation.org/media-center/press-release/americans-bedrooms-are-key-better-sleep-according-new-poll

# Sourcebook

## Mental health and wellbeing

**www.lifecoach-directory.org.uk**
For comprehensive data base of UK life coaches and NLP
   practitioners
**www.marymeadows.co.uk**
Life coach and NLP Practitioner
**www.mind.org.uk**
**www.sleepfoundation.org**
**www.ted.com/talks**
For TED Talks – influential videos by expert speakers

## Eco-friendly cleaning products

**www.biodegradable.biz**
**www.ecoegg.com**
**www.ecover.com**
**www.koala.eco**
**www.koh.com**
**www.methodproducts.co.uk**
**www.tincturelondon.com**

## Essential oils

**www.hollandandbarrett.com**
For 100 per cent pure essential oils
**www.nealsyardremedies.com**
For 100 per cent pure organic essential oils

## Donating

**www.ageuk.org.uk**
Charity shops and for computers, tablets, mobile phones,
    tools
**www.battersea.org.uk**
For bedding
**www.beautybank.org**
For unopened beauty products, toiletries and other 'little
    luxuries'
**www.bhf.org.uk** (British Heart Foundation)
Charity shops and for furniture – will collect from your home
**www.books2africa.org**
For books
**www.carolinehirons.com**
For Give and Make Up for unused make-up and cosmetics
**www.charitychoice.co.uk**
For list of all UK charities
**www.charityretail.org.uk**
To find charity shops in your area
**www.dogtrust.org.uk**
For bedding
**thedonkeysanctuary.org.uk**
For bedding
**www.emmaus.org.uk**
Charity shops and for furniture, electrical items, clothing, etc. –
    will collect from your home

**www.freecycle.org**
Nonprofit grassroots movement for donating and reusing stuff
for free in your town or neighbourhood
**www.thehygienebank.com**
For donating new, unused and in-date hygiene essentials,
beauty and personal care products
**www.lionsclubs.org/en**
For eyewear
**www.lovesupportunite.org**
For women's and girls' underwear
**www.mariecurie.org**
Charity shops and for eyewear
**www.nhs.uk**
For searching for hospitals to donate to waiting rooms,
children's wards and wards for elderly patients and for toys,
books, games
**www.oxfam.org.uk**
Charity shops
**www.redcross.org.uk**
Charity shops
**www.refuge.org.uk**
For clothes, toys and bedding
**www.rspca.org.uk**
For bedding
**www.salvationarmy.org.uk**
Charity shops and for toys, clothing
**www.savethechildren.org.uk**
Charity shops
**www.shelter.org.uk**
Charity shops and for clothing, furniture, books, electrical
items
**www.smallsforall.org**
For women's and girls' underwear
**www.specsavers.co.uk**
Accepts, recycles and donates eyewear working with specialist
charities

**www.tfsr.org** (Tools For Self Reliance)
For tools
**www.trusselltrust.org/get-help/find-a-foodbank/**
For food donations
**www.visionaidoverseas.org**
For eyewear
**www.womensaid.org.uk**
For clothes, toys, bedding, furniture
**www.workaid.org**
For tools
**www.ymca.org.uk**
For bedding, towels, linen, furniture

## Recycling

**www.compareandrecycle.co.uk**
For mobile phone recycling comparison
**www.sellmymobile.com**
For quotes from UK recycling companies
**www.terracycle.co.uk**
For recycling hard-to-recycle waste, as well as food wrappers,
    pens, plastic containers and bottles, etc.

# Acknowledgements

I want to begin by thanking HarperCollins for this amazing opportunity. I really did think you had the wrong email address when I saw you wanted me to write a book, and I'm so glad I didn't delete your message! Your constant support and 'you-can-do-it' attitude have really motivated me to stay calm and carry on. My special thanks to Carolyn, Omara, Jasmine and Rosie for helping me to create and achieve something special. Thank you for everything, you really are the best. And also thanks to Heather Thomas for helping me get the words down to meet the publishing schedule – I've never worked so fast!

. Thank you to my fabulous followers across social media. You are the reason I've written this book. If you had asked me two years ago whether this would happen, I would have stared back at you in complete amazement! To say I'm overwhelmed is an understatement. Every day, I'm so thankful for you all and pleased that I can share my love of organising. And knowing that it makes a difference to your homes and lives makes me so happy.

I would like to thank my dearest friends who've been right behind me, constantly pushing me on with This Girl Can Organise. They have helped and supported me, made me smile and guided me through the tough times, all the while believing in me and telling me I can achieve this. Just remember to always be NIC … I really adore you, girls. There are too many to mention and they know who they are but special thanks to my rocks: Julia, Pippa, Danielle, Annabel and Hannah.

Last, but certainly not least, a big thank you to my immediate family. Lottie, my beloved grandma – you won't get to read this, but I know you would have been overjoyed, proud and very emotional at seeing this achievement. See? I told you I was listening! Valerie, my fabulous mum and organising queen. By the way, this is all your fault (lol). Thank you for your everlasting support, guidance, constant love and always believing in me. I got to my happy place in the end. And Terry, the best daddy in the world. Thank you for always telling me to just 'go for it'. You are *the* kindest man I know, helping others, giving me your unconditional love and always working so hard for us all. This is why I've always looked up to you. I know you think this social media is bonkers, but trust me – this time next year, Rodders! My 'sister sister' Keeley: you've been endlessly patient with my publishing emails full of silly questions, but I'd be lost without you, love you. Also, my sister-in-law, Sarah, and in-laws, Chris and Raymond – for your love, constant support and advice. I am forever grateful.

My two gorgeous girls, Amelia and Francesca, thank you for your patience, love and support. I know a few things have lapsed recently and the routines have been a bit wobbly, but life is more exciting when you mix it up a bit. I am so super-proud of you, your independence, your 'can-do' attitudes and everything you set out to achieve. Mummy loves you both so much.

Graham, my love, my best friend. Thank you for loving me, supporting me and sharing this adventure with me. The last few months have been super-crazy bonkers, and even though this recent journey has been overwhelming, you have kept me calm, taken over the house, managed the kids and encouraged me every single day to just follow my vision and go for it. You always give me the freedom and flexibility to do what makes me happy. The last two years have been extremely challenging in so many ways, but you will always be my rock and I couldn't have done any of this without you. I love you.

Team work makes the dream work, folks, and thank goodness for you all …

# Index

# Index